ADVANCED HOME BAKING

Cream Puffs, page 50

ADVANCED
Home Baking

Recipes for Mastering Sweet & Savory Bakes

Jaclyn Rodriguez

Photography by Laura Flippen

ROCKRIDGE
PRESS

For general information on our other products and services or to obtain technical support, please contact our Customer Care Department within the United States at (866) 744-2665, or outside the United States at (510) 253-0500.

Rockridge Press publishes its books in a variety of electronic and print formats. Some content that appears in print may not be available in electronic books, and vice versa.

Interior and Cover Designer: Stephanie Mautone
Art Producer: Michael Hardgrove
Editor: Rebecca Markley
Production Editor: Andrew Yackira
Photography © 2020 Laura Flippen

ISBN: Print 978-1-64611-863-2 | eBook 978-1-64611-864-9
R0

For all those who chose passion over practicality, for those who are still dreaming of doing something special . . . this is for you.

Contents

Introduction

For as long as I can remember, anything creative has called to my soul. Art has always been a huge part of my life. As soon as I was old enough to be in the kitchen, I discovered that baking was another art form that I instantly loved. My mom has never been a fan of cooking, so she was always happy to have me as her little sous chef—and that's how I learned to cook.

Although I began my career as a visual artist, I've always had a special love for baking. I was the one everyone counted on to bring dessert to parties, and every time I was assigned the task, I would try to outdo what I had done last time. Years later, I took a leap and graduated first in my class in professional pastry from the famed International Culinary Center in New York City. I went on to work for many bakeries in the city, including the cake studio of world-renowned cake designer Ron Ben-Israel, where I was able to hone my skills and experience the joys—and, let's be honest, challenges—of working in New York City kitchens.

It was my continuing love of art and cakes that eventually led me to start my own cake business, Cake Designs by Jaclyn. Nothing makes me happier than creating a beautiful piece of edible art to commemorate a special occasion, to celebrate one of life's milestones, or to simply end a delicious meal with something sweet.

Throughout this book, I will teach you tips and techniques to create some of the most delicious, awe-inspiring breads and desserts, all from your home kitchen. Whether it's a two-foot-tall French croquembouche or fudge brownies, the recipes in this book will invite you to push your baking skills to the next level. Together, we will explore the complexities of flavor combinations and troubleshoot mistakes (trust me, I've made them all), and I will give you the insight and knowledge you need to bake like a pro. So, grab your kitchen scale and apron, and let's get ready to bake.

Chapter One

Next-Level Baking

It's no secret that baking can be challenging. How many times have you heard, "Oh, I love to cook! It's baking I can't do"? The fact is, baking is a science. It's all about precise measurements, chemistry, and a lot of patience. This may be intimidating to some people, but you already know the basics. Baking isn't that hard as long as you measure precisely and follow the recipe instructions. Baking successfully requires only the knowledge of how certain ingredients and cooking methods work. That's it! In most cases, you will be using a short list of basic ingredients, including flour, eggs, liquids (like milk or water), fat, sugar, and leavening agents, like baking powder or baking soda. With those simple ingredients, you can create the most delicious and complex confectionary delights.

Mirror Glaze, page 106 (left), decorated with abstract chocolate designs, chocolate shavings, and edible pearls

How Baking Actually Works

It's important to understand how certain ingredients and cooking methods work. Let's break down some of the science.

- **Formation and Expansion of Gases:** This is how the dough rises, through either chemical, organic, or mechanical leavening. Chemical leavening uses the gases released when ingredients like baking powder or baking soda are mixed with liquids, while organic leavening utilizes the gases given off by activated yeast. Mechanical leavening results from moisture and fats in the dough creating steam when they're heated, causing the dough to rise.

- **Trapped Gases in Air Cells:** The protein in the dough creates elastic webs to trap air, preventing them from being completely released and ensuring a light and airy baked good. When all the gases escape, baked goods will usually come out of the oven flatter and denser.

- **Coagulation of Proteins:** This refers to proteins in the dough becoming solids, which creates structure in baked goods. In order for this process to take place, it's important that your oven be set to the temperature listed in the recipe.

- **Evaporation of Water:** As previously mentioned, water or moisture evaporates throughout the baking process, creating steam and puffing up the dough or batter in a process known as mechanical leavening.

- **Melting Fats:** When fats melt, they release moisture, which aids mechanical leavening.

- **Crust Formation, Browning, and Caramelization:** As moisture is released, it evaporates, causing the surface of the dough to dry out and any sugars present to caramelize. This creates the brown, crispy crust we aim for in many baked goods.

Flour

Flour provides structure and foundation in baked goods. The gluten in flour is made up of predominantly two proteins: glutenin and gliadin. When these proteins bind together with moisture and heat, the gluten starts to develop and creates those elastic webs that trap air and gas to aid in leavening. There are many kinds of flours. What makes them different is the amount of protein each one contains. Protein is what determines how much gluten will develop, which is why you always want to make sure you're using the correct flour.

Cake Flour (5 to 8 percent protein)

Predominantly used for making cakes and sponges, this flour has the least amount of protein, which results in a fluffy, light crumb.

All-Purpose Flour (9 to 12 percent protein)

Commonly referred to as "AP flour," this is the flour that is most often found in our homes—and for good reason. It's the flour that usually appears in most baking and many other kinds of recipes. Be careful to use the specific flour called for in a recipe, though, and don't just substitute with this one.

Bread Flour (12 to 13 percent protein)

This type of flour has a higher percentage of protein, which allows for more gluten to develop, giving us that chewy texture and airy crumb we look forward to every time.

Almond Flour

For a gluten-free option, almond flour is a fantastic choice to create body and structure in pastry. It's made from finely ground, raw, unsalted almonds. I actually like to make my own almond flour by grinding almonds in a food processor for 2 to 3 minutes. Remember to store almond flour in an airtight container in the refrigerator to help it last longer.

Eggs

A very important ingredient in baking, eggs add moisture to doughs and batters, aid in leavening the product, and provide additional protein to help with structure. The fat in the yolk of the egg helps create a light and tender texture while providing a richer flavor. The yolk also has the ability to act as an emulsifier, preventing liquids and fats from separating.

Liquids

It's hard to imagine any kind of batter or dough without some sort of liquid. Liquids bind ingredients together, provide moisture to aid in leavening, and create a moist texture for a nice mouthfeel. Hydration from liquids such as whole milk or water is required for proteins to develop and create structure and texture. Think of liquids as the glue that brings everything together.

Water

Water is the universal liquid used in most baking. While it obviously helps bind together ingredients, much more than that happens during the mixing and baking process. Water assists in creating gluten to provide structure and texture. While baking, water evaporates and creates steam, aiding the mechanical leavening process. Water sometimes needs to be a certain temperature, such as when a recipe calls for lukewarm water to activate yeast.

Milk

Milk provides a lot of the same qualities water does; however, it also adds flavor. The fat and sugar in milk improve tenderness and texture in dough or batter. The sugar in the milk also adds to the development of a crust and browning in pastries. The basic rule is to use whole milk whenever a recipe calls for milk (unless it specifies something else or mentions a substitution), but if all you have is 2 percent or 1 percent, that will work just fine.

Fats

Fats contribute a huge amount of flavor and tenderness to your pastries. Fats coat the protein molecules and form a sort of barrier that keeps the gluten strands shorter, preventing them from overdeveloping. This results in a tender, moist, and often flaky pastry. Fats—especially solid fats, like butter and shortening—play a role in the leavening of your pastry by creating steam and pushing layers apart.

Butter

The most obvious role butter plays in baking is adding flavor. The richness gives your pastries or bread a very distinct and made-from-scratch taste. Butter aids in mechanical leavening, as well. Think of all those buttery layers in croissants or puff pastry: As soon as the butter heats up, it creates steam that allows those layers to puff right up. As a general rule, whenever you bake, you should be using unsalted butter. This allows you to control the salt content going into your food. The recipes in this book all call for unsalted butter. As a serious baker, you should ideally keep unsalted butter in your refrigerator or freezer at all times.

Oil

The main function of liquid fat, such as vegetable oil or canola oil, is to provide tenderness and richness. Because oils don't solidify when cooled, they will keep your baked goods moist and contribute to a really soft mouthfeel.

Shortening

Often interchangeable with butter, shortening behaves in a similar way and can provide the same results. Like butter, shortening is 100 percent fat, so it's able to produce an extremely tender and flaky product. By using shortening, you're also able to extend the shelf life of whatever you are baking.

Sugar

The first word you associate with pastry is most likely *sugar*. You can't really call something a pastry or dessert if it's not sweet, right? Probably the number-one function of sugar in your confections is to sweeten them, to provide that distinct flavor that we all look for when sinking our teeth into a cookie or a slice of cake. Like most ingredients, however, sugar has multiple duties. Sugar makes your baked goods tender by helping prohibit the development of too much gluten. Sugar is also hydroscopic, which means it helps hold on to moisture, and it aids in caramelization and browning to give your treats a great crust.

Granulated Sugar

The most common sugar used in baking, this is probably the variety you always keep in your pantry. Also known as "white sugar" or "regular sugar," it's the sugar with the largest crystal formation. This is the type of sugar used to sweeten the base of doughs and batters.

Brown Sugar

Whether it's light or dark, brown sugar is another sugar commonly used in baking and one you probably already have in your pantry. Brown sugar owes its distinctive color and deeper, rich flavor to the addition of molasses, which helps you achieve an even more pronounced browning effect during baking.

Confectioners' Sugar

Also known as "powdered sugar" or "icing sugar," confectioners' sugar is finely ground granulated sugar. This type of sugar is perfect for adding to frostings or icings because of its ability to melt into whatever you're mixing it into. It's also a wonderful ingredient for decorating pastries and desserts. A light sprinkle can totally elevate your presentation.

Leavening Agents

There are many different ways to leaven your baked goods, including baking powder and baking soda, which are considered chemical leaveners; yeast, which is an organic leavener; and air and steam, which are mechanical leaveners. All these substances cause a reaction in your dough or batter, helping it to rise and puff up. It's worth noting that not all leaveners are created equal and they are not interchangeable. You must pay attention to which specific leavener is called for in a recipe. I made the mistake of using baking soda instead of baking powder when making blueberry muffins once, and I got green muffins rather than blue ones!

Chemical Leaveners

The most common chemical leaveners are baking soda and baking powder. These are the agents that, when added to a dough or batter, work by reacting with water, salt, acid (such as lemon juice), and other ingredients to produce carbon dioxide. This then causes the lift in pastry and bread doughs. Baking soda is much stronger than baking powder, and it requires acid, such as yogurt, sour cream, vinegar, or lemon juice, to react. Baking powder contains two forms of acid that allow it to react at different times during the baking process: once when it comes into contact with a wet batter and again when it is heated.

Organic Leaveners

Yeast is the prime example of an organic leavener. Like the chemical leaveners mentioned before, yeast aids in the development of the dough by beginning the process of fermentation. Fermentation begins when the yeast feeds off the sugar present in the dough and releases carbon dioxide as a by-product. Just like with chemical leaveners, carbon dioxide is what causes lift and expansion in your doughs and batters.

Mechanical Leavening

Mechanical leavening is almost always present in any kind of dough or batter you're creating. It's achieved by incorporating air into the product by whisking (think of a fluffy meringue) or through folding the dough (as with croissants or puff pastry). It's also achieved by producing steam. Think about puff pastry, with all of those buttery layers that begin to release moisture and create steam as soon as they hit the oven. This is what causes the layers to separate and puff up.

Advanced Kitchen Essentials

As an advanced home baker, it's necessary to acquire certain kitchen tools and specialized ingredients to produce a consistent pastry product. At first glance, they may not seem essential, but I promise that when you see the results of your bakes, you'll realize they are worth the investment.

Tools

While it's easy to get carried away and want to purchase everything you see in the local Williams Sonoma store (guilty!), the following is a list of items I think every advanced home baker should have in their arsenal.

Digital Kitchen Scale

I can't express how important it is to have a scale and to weigh your ingredients. With this method, there is very little room for error. Let's face it, how many of us have the exact same measuring cup set? What is the standard measurement for a "heap"? When you weigh your ingredients, it takes all the guesswork out of the equation. There are plenty of options out there, so you don't need to spend a lot of money. Truth be told, while I did eventually splurge on a rather expensive one, I find that I keep going back to this hilariously bright orange, very inexpensive scale that I got in culinary school, and it's become my tried-and-true scale. All the recipes in this book call for ingredients to be measured by weight using metric units, so be sure to always weigh your ingredients in grams.

If You Don't Have a Stand Mixer

While a stand mixer certainly can make life in the kitchen easier, it's not totally necessary. Think about it. What did people do hundreds of years ago? A little bit of elbow grease and a wooden spoon is all it took. All the recipes in this book can be accomplished by using an electric hand mixer or mixing by hand.

Most stand mixers come with several attachments, including a whisk, a paddle, and a hook, but you can use a hand whisk, a spatula, and your hands to replicate these attachments. Not only will you get a workout, but you'll also have a delicious dessert in the end. Sounds like a win-win to me!

Electric hand mixers can be inexpensive and often come with both whisk and "beater" attachments, so that could be a viable option if you have a small budget. While a stand mixer might be something you want to get in the future, you'll still be able to create these spectacular desserts by hand or with a simple hand mixer.

Candy Thermometer

A candy thermometer will come in handy when you're boiling sugar for meringues or when you're making candy like caramels. Temperature plays a huge role when you cook with sugar. Like weighing ingredients, precise temperatures can be an integral part of executing recipes.

Round Ring Molds

These are some of my favorite pieces of kitchen equipment because they're so versatile. Ring molds are great for making tarts, cutting cake pieces from a baking tray, or cutting out perfect circles of smoothed-out tempered chocolate. You'll even find yourself using them for several recipes in this book, including Buttermilk Biscuits (page 17) and Linzer Cookies (page 135). You can purchase a set of them in various sizes and use them to plate desserts or savory dishes.

Offset Spatula

Another one of my most used items, this is predominantly used for spreading frosting onto cakes, spreading batter evenly in a pan, or smoothing chocolate to create decorations. It's also important to have varying sizes. I have about 20 offset spatulas in a variety of sizes because I use them so much. What can I say? They make me happy!

Bench Scraper

Bench scrapers have multiple purposes in the pastry kitchen. They're really good for cutting butter into dough, transporting ingredients to a bowl or a saucepan, and scraping dough and sticky bits off your work surface.

Zester

This is a pretty crucial tool in pastry when you need to zest all those tart and tangy citrus fruits or grate spices like nutmeg into batter. You can even use a zester to shave down the edges of a cooked tart shell to make it more even.

Pastry Bags and Tips

Piping can be one of the more intimidating aspects of pastry, but once you practice a bit, you'll be a pro. Pastry bags (also called piping bags) and tips are not just for decorating cakes, though; they're also used for filling pastries and piping out batter (such as pâte à choux for Éclairs, page 54). You can buy sets of Ateco or Wilton tips so that you have a variety on hand.

Kitchen Torch

When you think of a kitchen torch, you probably think about using it to create that crispy caramelized top on a Crème Brûlée (page 69). It has lots of other uses in the kitchen, though, including toasting meringues and marshmallows and loosening a ring mold around a cold or frozen dessert.

Ingredients

Along with common staples, like granulated sugar and all-purpose flour, it's important for the advanced baker to have specialized ingredients readily available in the kitchen. The following is a list of ingredients that you'll begin to find yourself grabbing when you're looking to make that next "wow" dessert.

Gelatin

Gelatin is a great ingredient to keep on hand due to its ability to thicken any kind of filling (curds or creams, for example) or mousse. You can find gelatin in two forms: sheets and, more commonly, powder. I prefer the sheets because I find that they combine better into mixtures than the powdered varieties.

Corn Syrup

Corn syrup helps stabilize your mixture, aids in thickening, adds a softer texture, and prevents sugar crystals from forming. You'll find yourself reaching for the corn syrup when you're making any sort of candy or caramel.

Confectioners' Sugar

This type of sugar has become a staple in my kitchen for as long as I can remember. While it works perfectly for decoration, it's also the key ingredient in royal icing. A light dusting can make a Chocolate Soufflé (page 68) much more enticing, and it's a great sugar to use when making lighter batters, like Angel Food Cake (page 109) or Lady Fingers (page 52).

Vanilla Beans or Vanilla Bean Paste

There's nothing better than the taste, look (those little brown speckles are everything), and smell of fresh vanilla—one of my favorite ingredients. I'm not a huge fan of most store-bought vanilla extracts because I find they don't provide enough flavor, so instead I always scrape the seeds from a fresh vanilla bean or use 1 teaspoon of vanilla bean paste. Save scraped vanilla bean pods and soak three of them in 1 cup of vodka. Six months later and voilà! You've made your own vanilla extract. Keep adding empty pods as you use them and ⅓ cup of vodka as needed to replenish.

Cornstarch

Cornstarch is one of those things that you might already have in your kitchen but probably use only once or twice a year because you're not actually sure what to do with it. Cornstarch is a great ingredient to have on hand because of its thickening abilities. It's great to use in fruit compotes and pastry cream. Pastry cream powder, one of the main ingredients in pastry cream, is a product you can buy that is actually just cornstarch with vanilla flavoring.

Unsalted Butter

I'm pretty sure butter may be the most used ingredient in this book. Remember to always use unsalted butter so that you can control the amount of salt in a batter or dough. The amount of salt varies from brand to brand, so start off with a consistent base and add your salt according to taste.

Dark Chocolate

It's never a bad idea to have chocolate in your kitchen, but you especially need it when you're a baker. It's a staple ingredient to say the least, used in everything from mousse to soufflés. A good-quality chocolate with a high cocoa content makes all the difference. Your desserts will have a richer, more chocolaty taste and a very smooth mouthfeel.

Terminology

Throughout this book, you're going to see certain words and phrases repeated in the recipes. In order to expand your baking and pastry knowledge, it's important that you become familiar with these terms and eventually commit them to memory. At the very least, you'll have some fun baking facts to share at dinner parties. Note that some of these terms are redefined for you in the recipes.

Batard: a short loaf of bread in an oval or oblong shape

Blind baking: baking a pie shell or crust in the oven before filling it

Boule: a round loaf of crusty bread

Bulk ferment: to let dough go through a primary fermentation

Crème légère: a mixture of pastry cream and whipped cream

Cut in: to incorporate butter into flour until only small pieces of butter remain

Dock: to use a fork to pierce holes in dough to allow steam to escape during baking, such as when baking tart or pie shells

Fermentation: a process through which yeast and bacteria convert sugars into carbon dioxide (this is what causes dough to rise when using yeast)

Fold: to combine ingredients in a delicate manner so as not to deflate them, such as when folding whipped cream into pastry cream

Forming a ribbon: when the batter falls onto itself in a thickness that looks like a ribbon

Lame: a tool used to slice the tops of unbaked bread

Laminated dough: dough made up of many thin layers separated by butter, created by repeated rolling and folding

Macaronage: the process of mixing together your macaron ingredients to achieve a specific consistency

Pâte à choux: a light batter used to make pastries like éclairs or cream puffs, made only from eggs, butter, water, and flour

Poolish: a type of wet pre-ferment

Pre-ferment: a fermentation starter

Pulling a window: the process of taking a handful of dough and stretching it apart to check the gluten development of some doughs; if the dough is able to stretch so thin that you can see through it without it ripping, then you've developed enough gluten and you can proceed

Punch down: to use your hands to flatten a dough that has been proofed

Soaker: firm ingredients soaked in liquid to soften before being added to dough or batter

Sponge: a type of pre-ferment

Tangzhong: the starter used in Japanese Milk Bread (page 36)

Tempering eggs: adding a warm or hot liquid to your egg mixture a little at a time in order to not cook or scramble the eggs

About This Book

As you move forward into this book, you'll find that many recipes are broken down by components, including the dough, filling, and finishing. Some recipes may reference a previous recipe, which you can look up and complete before moving on. "Tips of the Trade" will help you along as you make the recipes. You'll find additional tips throughout the recipes that will help you with techniques, troubleshooting, substituting ingredients, serving ideas, and suggestions for upgrading a recipe to make it even more spectacular. Feel free to jump ahead and check out chapter 7 for decoration tips and tricks that will help give your finished cakes and pastries a professional touch.

Chapter Two

Breads and Rolls

Pretzel Rolls, page 34 (left)

Tips of the Trade

Bread baking can be time-consuming—many recipes require resting, proofing, and kneading—but I know you're up for the challenge. Honestly, it's totally doable and worth it, especially with the following tips.

Familiarize Yourself with the Dough

Practice really does make perfect when it comes to making bread. As you become more familiar with how the dough feels as you're kneading, you'll begin to automatically "feel" if the dough isn't right (it's too dry, too sticky, etc.). This is such an important ability to have when baking, especially when making bread. If the dough is too sticky, do not add more flour, even though that might seem to make sense. Instead, keep kneading! Adding too much flour will result in a crumbly loaf. If the dough is too dry and cracking, add water a few drops at a time until the dough comes together.

Watch the Oven

Bread is very much like a little kid: If you take your eye off of it for very long, who knows what trouble it can get into? A common mistake a lot of bakers make is throwing something in the oven (any kind of baked good, not just bread) and then forgetting about it until the timer goes off. You need to be proactive and check the bread several times to make sure it's not browning too quickly. If it is, rotate the pan in the oven and keep baking.

Take Notes

Bread can be very temperamental—even a slight change in weather or temperature in a room can alter the outcome of the bake. This is why I like to keep a little kitchen journal whenever I'm baking to jot down all the details, especially when I'm trying a new recipe. I note the weather that day, how long I let the dough rest, and so on. This is a great habit to get into, no matter what you're cooking. The next time someone asks what you want for your birthday, ask for a kitchen journal!

Score the Bread

This step is important to prevent the bread from splitting open and cracking during baking. Scoring or slashing the shaped dough before baking lets the dough spread out a bit without ripping before the "spring," which is the final burst of rising in the oven before the crust forms and hardens.

Plan and Be Patient

Bread baking requires a real time commitment. You must plan accordingly and allow yourself the time to let the dough rest, proof, chill, and ferment. You cannot rush these processes if you hope to achieve a solid result.

Irish Soda Bread, page 20

Corn Bread

Prep time: 10 minutes • **Cook time:** 25 to 30 minutes

When I was growing up, we had corn bread only on special occasions. Years later, I learned how easy it is to make and realized that I could have it whenever I want. Now it's one of my favorite breads to enjoy at breakfast, slathered with lots of butter. • *Yield: 2 (9-by-5-inch) loaves or 24 muffins*

Butter, for greasing the pans

225 grams all-purpose flour, plus more for dusting

335 grams granulated sugar

85 grams cornmeal

20 grams baking powder

1 teaspoon salt

3 large eggs

280 milliliters buttermilk

150 milliliters vegetable oil

Honey, for serving (optional)

1. Preheat the oven to 350°F. Butter and flour 2 (9-by-5-inch) loaf pans or 2 (12-cup) muffin pans and set aside.

2. In a large bowl, mix together the flour, sugar, cornmeal, baking powder, and salt.

3. Add the eggs, buttermilk, and vegetable oil and stir just to combine all ingredients. Do not overmix.

4. Pour the batter into the prepared pans.

5. Bake for 25 to 30 minutes, or until golden brown on the outside and a skewer inserted into the center comes out clean. Serve with a drizzle of honey on top (if using).

6. Store the corn bread wrapped tightly in plastic wrap in the refrigerator for up to 1 week or in the freezer for up to 3 months.

Troubleshooting Tip: The oil in this recipe gives the corn bread a longer shelf life by keeping it moist.

Upgrade Tip: Add layers of complexity to your corn bread by stirring in crumbled cooked bacon, shredded cheese, or chopped jalapeño peppers (or all three!) when mixing your wet and dry ingredients together.

Buttermilk Biscuits

Prep time: 15 minutes · **Cook time:** 10 to 12 minutes

There's something super comforting about a warm, buttery biscuit that can make anyone smile. It's a simple staple recipe that every dedicated home baker should have in their repertoire. With just a few simple ingredients, which you probably already have in your kitchen, you're just steps away from fluffy bliss. Spread warm biscuits with butter and jam, use them as a topping for a pot pie, or smother them with sausage gravy. · *Yield: 10 to 12 biscuits*

455 grams all-purpose flour, plus more for dusting

1 teaspoon salt

1 teaspoon baking powder

1 teaspoon baking soda

1 teaspoon sugar

170 grams cold unsalted butter, cubed

280 milliliters buttermilk

1. Preheat the oven to 400°F. Line a sheet pan with parchment paper and set aside.

2. In a large bowl, whisk together the flour, salt, baking powder, baking soda, and sugar.

3. Transfer the flour mixture onto a clean work surface and, using a bench scraper, cut in the butter cubes until they are pea-size.

4. Create a well in the middle of the flour mixture. Slowly add the buttermilk while using the bench scraper to blend the ingredients together. The dough should still be sticky once everything is combined. Do not overmix. You should still see chunks of butter throughout the dough.

5. Lightly flour the work surface and the dough, and knead the dough 10 to 12 times.

6. Gently pat the dough out to about 1 inch thick and, using a biscuit cutter or a glass, cut out 10 biscuits. Be careful not to twist the biscuit cutter when cutting the dough or the biscuits may not rise properly. Gently place the biscuits on the sheet pan, spacing them about 1 inch apart. Pat out any leftover dough to get 1 or 2 more biscuits.

7. Bake for 10 to 12 minutes, or until golden brown. Let cool on a wire rack.

Serving Tip: These are best served warm fresh out of the oven, brushed with melted salted butter.

Scones

Prep time: 10 minutes • Cook time: 10 to 15 minutes

Another breakfast favorite of mine, scones are a great vehicle for experimenting with flavors. They also come together very quickly and are a good choice if you're throwing together a last-minute brunch. • *Yield: 12 to 15 scones*

325 grams all-purpose flour, plus more for dusting

50 grams granulated sugar

20 grams baking powder

¼ teaspoon salt

1 large egg

1 large egg yolk

130 milliliters heavy cream, plus more for brushing

110 grams cold unsalted butter, cubed

100 grams raisins or currants

1. Preheat the oven to 350°F. Line a sheet pan with parchment paper and set aside.

2. In a large bowl, whisk together the flour, sugar, baking powder, and salt.

3. In a small bowl, whisk together the egg, egg yolk, and heavy cream.

4. Transfer the flour mixture to a clean work surface. Using a bench scraper, cut in the butter cubes until they are pea-size.

5. Add the raisins to the flour mixture and stir to combine.

6. Add the egg mixture to the flour mixture and stir just until a dough forms, being careful not to overmix. It should be slightly sticky and soft.

7. Flour the work surface and gently roll or pat out the dough to about ¾ inch thick.

8. Cut the dough into your desired shape (circles, squares, or my favorite, triangles). Place them on the sheet pan and brush lightly with heavy cream.

9. Bake for 10 to 15 minutes, until lightly browned. Let cool on a wire rack.

10. Store leftovers in an airtight container at room temperature for up to 2 days or wrapped tightly in plastic wrap in the freezer for up to 2 months.

Upgrade Tip: Some of my favorite variations include the addition of about 100 grams of chocolate chips, cinnamon chips, or blueberries or the zest of 1 orange for a sweet scone. You could also add 50 grams of minced chives and 4 slices of crumbled cooked bacon or 50 grams of grated Parmesan cheese for something savory. Feel free to experiment. Any additional ingredients should go into the flour mixture in step 5.

Irish Soda Bread

Prep time: 10 minutes • **Cook time:** 30 to 40 minutes

This quick bread has about the same texture as a scone, and the perfect accompaniment would be a little butter and jam. Traditional recipes often include raisins, and here I've also added caraway seeds, which give it a subtle anise flavor. The "soda" in this bread is baking soda, which reacts with the buttermilk and helps the bread rise while baking. I'm sure many of us have enjoyed this bread around St. Patrick's Day, but I think it's too delicious to relegate to just once a year. • *Yield: 1 boule*

390 grams all-purpose flour,
   plus more for dusting

50 grams granulated sugar

1½ teaspoons baking soda

1 teaspoon salt

25 grams cold unsalted
   butter, cubed

110 grams raisins or currants

1 tablespoon caraway seeds

1 tablespoon orange
   zest (optional)

280 milliliters buttermilk

1. Preheat the oven to 350°F. Line a sheet pan with parchment paper and set aside.

2. In a large bowl, whisk together the flour, sugar, baking soda, and salt.

3. Using a pastry cutter or two knives, cut in the cold butter until you have a coarse crumb. Add the raisins, caraway seeds, and orange zest (if using) and mix to combine.

4. Add the buttermilk and mix just until combined. Do not overmix.

5. Transfer the dough to a clean, lightly floured work surface and shape the dough into a ball. Using a paring knife, cut a shallow, large "X" across the top of the dough.

6. Transfer the dough to the prepared sheet pan and bake for 30 to 40 minutes, until browned.

Troubleshooting Tip: If your bread is browning too quickly, place an aluminum foil tent over the bread and continue to bake. Brush off any burned raisins from the surface.

Cheese Straws

Prep time: 15 minutes • Cook time: 15 to 20 minutes

One of my favorite things to do with leftover puff pastry is to make these cheese straws. They're the perfect addition to any charcuterie board or platter of appetizers as well as a delicious anytime snack. They're super versatile, which also makes them fun to experiment with by switching out seasonings to change the flavors. • *Yield: 25 to 30 straws*

½ recipe Puff Pastry (page 48)

150 grams Parmesan cheese

Paprika, for dusting

1. Line a sheet pan with parchment paper.

2. Roll the puff pastry into a rectangle about ½ inch thick.

3. Lightly brush with water, being careful not to make the dough soggy. Sprinkle the Parmesan cheese over the top. Lightly sprinkle with paprika.

4. Using a rolling pin, gently roll over the cheese and paprika to make them adhere to the dough.

5. Using a large knife or a pastry wheel, cut ½-inch-wide strips starting from the shorter side of the rectangle, making sure not to drag the knife through the dough. Instead, use a slicing motion to get clean lines.

6. Twist one of the strips of dough a few times and place it on the prepared sheet pan. Repeat with the rest of the strips. Place the pan in the refrigerator to chill for about 10 minutes.

7. Preheat the oven to 350°F.

8. Bake for 15 to 20 minutes, or until golden brown. Let cool on a wire rack.

9. Cheese straws are best the same day they're made, so enjoy them right away!

Substitution Tip: Use 150 grams of any kind of semi-hard to hard cheese, such as Romano, Asiago, or sharp cheddar. Instead of paprika, try sprinkling with garlic powder, dried thyme, dried oregano, Italian seasoning, chili powder, or onion powder for a different flavor. Or try a mixture of 1 part cinnamon and 2 parts sugar for something sweet.

Troubleshooting Tip: You may notice that some of the cheese will fall off when you twist the strips of dough. Don't worry—after twisting and placing the strips on the sheet pan, you can sprinkle a little more cheese over each strip before you put them in the oven.

Focaccia

Prep time: 3 hours 45 minutes • **Cook time:** 12 to 15 minutes

Depending on what you decide to add to this, focaccia can almost be a meal on its own. It's deliciously oily and crusty and is a sure-fire hit with any crowd. I love it so much that I may or may not have been known to eat a whole tray on my own (shhhh, don't tell anyone). • *Yield: 1 (18-by-13-inch) focaccia*

11 grams instant dry yeast

¼ teaspoon granulated sugar

635 milliliters warm
water, divided

850 grams bread flour, plus
more for dusting

220 milliliters olive oil, divided,
plus more for greasing
the bowl

1 tablespoon kosher salt

Optional toppings

Grated Parmesan, shredded
cheddar, or grated
Asiago cheese

Fresh chopped rosemary, fresh
thyme, dried basil, dried chili
flakes, dried oregano

Chopped walnuts, sliced or
slivered almonds, pine nuts

Flaky sea salt

Balsamic vinegar

Honey

1. In a small bowl, mix together the yeast, sugar, and 45 milliliters of warm water. Set the yeast aside to activate until it begins to bubble up, about 5 minutes.

2. In the bowl of a stand mixer fitted with the paddle attachment, combine the remaining 590 milliliters of warm water, the flour, 110 milliliters of olive oil, and the salt. Add the activated yeast mixture and, starting at the lowest speed, beat for about 1 minute, just to combine. Increase the speed to medium and beat for 3 to 5 minutes, until a dough forms.

3. Oil a large bowl and set aside.

4. Transfer the dough to a lightly floured work surface, knead 1 or 2 times, and form it into a ball. Place the dough in the oiled bowl and cover with plastic wrap. Let the dough proof in a warm area until it has doubled in size, about 2 hours.

5. Line a sheet pan with parchment paper and pour the remaining 110 milliliters of olive oil into the pan.

6. When the dough has finished proofing, gently stretch the dough out to fit the pan. Use a light hand to avoid deflating the dough, which will result in a dense focaccia.

7. Make dimples in the dough with your fingertips and add whatever toppings you'd like. Cover with a kitchen towel and proof the dough for another 30 minutes in a warm place.

8. Preheat the oven to 425°F.

Caramelized onions

Minced garlic

Olives

Crumbled cooked bacon

Grapes

Peach slices

Strawberry slices

Sliced tomatoes

9. Bake for 12 to 15 minutes, or until golden brown. Cut into slices and serve warm.

10. Store leftover focaccia in an airtight container at room temperature for up to 2 days or wrap tightly in plastic wrap and freeze for up to 1 month.

Upgrade Tip: Here are my favorite combinations for toppings:

- Sliced strawberries and balsamic drizzle
- Sliced tomatoes, minced garlic, and grated Parmesan
- Chopped fresh rosemary, sea salt, and grapes
- Grated Asiago, bacon crumbles, and honey drizzle
- Olives, minced garlic, and oregano

Seeded Multigrain Sandwich Bread

Prep time: 2 days　•　**Cook time:** 30 minutes

I always feel a little less guilty about my carb intake when I reach for a slice of this bread, because eating multigrain bread counts as being healthy, right? I love the texture it offers, from the chewy oats to the crunchy seeds. It's a really nice bread to have on hand, whether it's for toast in the morning or a delicious afternoon sandwich. 　•　*Yield: 2 (9-by-5-inch) loaves*

For the soaker

25 grams flaxseed

25 grams sesame seeds

25 grams poppy seeds

25 grams sunflower seeds

25 grams pumpkin seeds

25 grams chopped walnuts or pecans (optional)

50 grams chopped dried fruit (optional)

For the poolish

65 grams bread flour

Pinch instant dry yeast

65 milliliters water

For the dough

Vegetable oil, for greasing the bowl

Extra seeds, for rolling

415 grams bread flour

180 grams whole-wheat flour

30 grams rolled oats

20 grams cornmeal

20 grams honey or brown sugar

20 grams salt

1 teaspoon instant dry yeast

390 milliliters water

Day 1

1. **To make the soaker:** In a medium bowl, mix together the flaxseed, sesame seeds, poppy seeds, sunflower seeds, pumpkin seeds, walnuts (if using), and fruit (if using). Cover with plastic wrap and set aside at room temperature.

2. **To make the poolish:** In a medium bowl, mix together the bread flour, yeast, and water. Cover with plastic wrap and set aside at room temperature for 15 to 18 hours.

Day 2

1. Oil a large bowl. In a separate large, shallow bowl, mix together additional seeds of your choice and set aside.

2. **To make the dough:** In the bowl of a stand mixer fitted with the paddle attachment, combine the bread flour, whole-wheat flour, oats, cornmeal, honey, salt, yeast, water, and the poolish and mix on low speed for about 2 minutes, until just combined.

3. Increase to high speed and mix for about 5 minutes, until a dough starts to form.

4. Add the soaker and mix until thoroughly combined.

5. Place the dough in the oiled bowl to bulk ferment until it doubles in size, about 1 hour.

6. Grease 2 (9-by-5-inch) loaf pans.

7. On a clean work surface, divide the dough in half and shape into two rounds. Let the dough rest for 15 minutes.

8. Shape each round of dough into a log, roll them in the extra seed mixture, and place them into the prepared loaf pans, seam-side down. Cover with a kitchen towel and proof in a warm place until nearly doubled in size, about 1 hour.

9. Preheat the oven to 400°F.

10. Bake for 30 minutes, or until browned on top. Let the loaves cool in the pans for a few minutes before removing and cooling completely on a wire rack.

11. To store, wrap each loaf tightly in plastic wrap at room temperature for up to 3 days or for up to 3 months in the freezer.

Serving Tip: Double the recipe and freeze two of the loaves for later.

Pizza

Prep time: 1 hour 20 minutes · **Cook time:** 15 to 20 minutes

As a native New Yorker—particularly as a Manhattanite—I take my pizza very seriously. Let's face it, pizza is all about the crust: It can't be too thick or too thin, and it needs just the right amount of crispiness and chew to it. Whether you're making a simple cheese pizza or a fancy gourmet version with blue cheese and pears, a great pizza always starts with a great crust. · *Yield: 2 (12-inch) pizzas*

Cornmeal, for dusting

Vegetable oil, for greasing the bowl

500 grams bread flour, plus more for dusting

300 milliliters water, at room temperature

10 grams instant dry yeast

5 grams sugar

5 grams salt

Optional toppings

Your favorite sauce

Shredded mozzarella

1. Preheat the oven to 425°F. Line one large or two small sheet pans with parchment paper and dust lightly with cornmeal. Set aside. Oil a large bowl and set aside.

2. In the bowl of a stand mixer fitted with the paddle attachment, combine the flour, water, yeast, sugar, and salt. Mix on low speed until it forms a soft dough, about 3 minutes.

3. Form the dough into a smooth round ball and place it into the oiled bowl. Cover with plastic wrap and proof until it's doubled in size, about 1 hour.

4. Turn the dough out onto a clean floured work surface and divide into two equal pieces. Let the dough rest for 10 to 15 minutes.

5. Shape and stretch each piece of dough into 2 (12-inch) discs and place them on the sheet pan(s). Top with sauce, shredded mozzarella, and any desired toppings (see Serving Tip).

6. Bake the pizzas for 15 to 20 minutes, or until the bottom and edges are nicely browned and the toppings are cooked or melted.

7. If not baking right away, place each raw ball of dough in a zip-top plastic bag—this will leave room for the dough to continue to proof and grow a little bit more—and refrigerate for up to 3 days or freeze for up to 1 month. Place frozen dough in the refrigerator in the morning to defrost and use that evening.

Serving Tip: Some of my favorite toppings include mushrooms, pepperoni, olives, green peppers, sausage, basil, and fresh mozzarella. Any toppings should be added right before baking your pizza. Create your own personal pizza with your favorites. Did somebody say pizza party?

Vienna Bread

Prep time: 3 hours • **Cook time:** 10 to 12 minutes

This type of bread is absolutely perfect for making delicious sandwiches because it's softer than a traditional baguette and has a slightly sweeter flavor. It's also lovely to just split open, toast, and enjoy with some butter and jam. • *Yield: 2 loaves*

Oil, for greasing the bowl
125 milliliters milk
110 grams bread flour
42 grams unsalted butter, at
  room temperature
15 grams milk powder
12 grams granulated sugar
5 grams instant dry yeast
5 grams salt
1 large egg, beaten,
  for egg wash

1. Line a sheet pan with parchment paper. Oil a large bowl and set aside.

2. In the bowl of a stand mixer fitted with the paddle attachment, combine the milk, bread flour, butter, milk powder, sugar, yeast, and salt and mix on low speed for 2 minutes. Switch to the dough hook attachment and mix on medium-high speed until the dough has come together and is fully combined, 8 minutes.

3. Place the dough in the oiled bowl and proof until the dough has doubled in size, 1 hour.

4. Divide the dough in half and shape the pieces into batards (see Technique Tip). Place them on the prepared sheet pan and let rest for 10 minutes.

5. Brush the dough with the beaten egg wash and score the baguettes with a sharp knife diagonally along the length of the loaf. Proof until the dough puffs up and jiggles slightly when you shake the pan, about 1 hour 30 minutes.

6. Preheat the oven to 375°F.

7. Brush the dough once more with the egg wash and bake for 10 to 12 minutes, or until golden brown.

8. The loaves can be stored in an airtight container at room temperature for up to 2 days or frozen for up to 1 month.

Technique Tips:

- *No stand mixer?* If you don't have a stand mixer, mix the ingredients in a large bowl until combined. Turn out the dough mixture onto a lightly floured work surface and knead until the dough is smooth and pliable, 12 to 15 minutes.
- *What's a batard?* Batards are like baguettes but with tapered ends instead of more squared-off ends.

Brioche

Prep time: 2 days • **Cook time:** 30 to 40 minutes

Brioche is an enriched bread with a high butter and egg content, which makes it decadent enough to make you feel like you're eating dessert. I love to use it in bread pudding or, even better, French toast. Brioche rolls are also nice to dress up a sandwich or to have alongside a special holiday dinner. • *Yield: 2 (9-by-5-inch) loaves*

Vegetable oil, for greasing
   the bowl
170 grams cold unsalted butter
125 milliliters milk, at
   room temperature
10 grams instant dry yeast
500 grams bread flour
200 grams eggs (see Technique
   Tip), plus 1 large egg, beaten,
   for egg wash
70 grams sugar
10 grams salt

Day 1

1. Oil a large bowl.

2. Using a rolling pin, temper the butter by pounding it on a clean work surface until it's softened. Return the butter to the refrigerator until ready to use.

3. In a small bowl, mix together the milk and yeast. Let stand for 5 minutes, until foamy.

4. In the bowl of a stand mixer fitted with the paddle attachment, combine the flour, 200 grams of eggs, and the yeast mixture on low speed for about 2 minutes.

5. Add the sugar and salt and beat for 1 minute.

6. Switch to the hook attachment and mix on high speed until the gluten develops, 5 to 6 minutes.

   PRO TIP: To check if the gluten has developed, you can "pull a window" by taking a handful of the dough and stretching it apart. If you can stretch the dough so thin that you can see through it (like a window) without it ripping, then you're good to go.

7. Switch back to the paddle attachment and, with the mixer on low speed, add the tempered butter a piece at a time and mix until the dough is very smooth and almost shiny. You will have to continuously scrape dough off the paddle and the sides of the bowl during the mixing process. You'll know the dough is finished mixing when it completely pulls away from the bowl on its own and is very smooth. This can sometimes take a long time, so if the dough is still shaggy and not coming together, keep mixing.

8. Place the finished dough in the oiled bowl, cover in plastic wrap, and bulk ferment for about 1 hour. Punch the dough down and shape into a ball. Wrap in plastic wrap and place in the refrigerator overnight.

Day 2

1. Grease 2 (9-by-5-inch) loaf pans.

2. Divide the dough into two equal pieces, shape into logs, and place into the loaf pans, seam-side down.

3. Brush the dough with the beaten egg, cover with a kitchen towel, and let proof in a warm place until almost doubled in size, about 2 hours.

4. If not using right away, store raw dough wrapped in plastic in the refrigerator for up to 2 days or in the freezer for up to 1 week. Place frozen dough in the refrigerator to defrost for about 1 hour before using.

5. To bake, preheat the oven to 350°F.

6. Brush another layer of egg wash on top of the dough. Bake for 30 to 40 minutes, or until the bread is golden brown and sounds hollow when tapped.

7. Remove the loaves from the pans and let cool on a wire rack.

Technique Tips:

- *Tempering butter.* It's quite common in French pastry to "temper" butter. To do this, pound cold butter with a rolling pin to soften it and then return it to the refrigerator until you are ready to use it. This helps the butter blend smoothly into the dough.
- *Kneading dough.* It's important to knead the dough and develop the gluten properly before adding the butter, because butter inhibits gluten development.
- *Weighing eggs.* In this recipe, the eggs are weighed. To get the right amount, first crack an egg into a bowl set on a kitchen scale and add eggs until you get close to the amount you need. Then, crack 1 egg in a separate bowl and whisk briefly. Pour the egg slowly into the bowl with the other eggs until you reach the weight specified in your recipe.

Troubleshooting Tip: If you do not have a stand mixer, you can mix the dough by hand, then knead it on a clean, floured work surface for 10 to 15 minutes. "Pull a window" to check for gluten development and proceed with the recipe.

English Muffins

Prep time: 2 hours · **Cook time:** 5 to 7 minutes

I never thought about actually making my own English muffins before I went to culinary school. I mean, why bother when you can grab perfectly good ones right off the shelf at the grocery store? But once I learned to make them, it gave me a strong sense of accomplishment, and it really wows people when you say, "These English muffins are homemade." Even better—homemade English muffins are completely delicious! · *Yield: 12 to 15 muffins*

Sponge

Oil, for greasing the bowl
150 grams all-purpose flour
10 grams instant dry yeast
125 milliliters water

Dough

350 grams all-purpose flour,
    plus more for dusting
200 milliliters milk
15 grams unsalted butter,
    plus 2 tablespoons
10 grams salt
Cornmeal, for dusting
2 tablespoons oil

To make the sponge

1. Oil a large bowl and set aside.

2. In a medium bowl, mix together the flour, yeast, and water and let sit for at least 20 minutes.

To make the dough and cook the muffins

1. Transfer the sponge to the bowl of a stand mixer fitted with the paddle attachment. Add the flour, milk, 15 grams of butter, and salt and mix on low speed for about 2 minutes.

2. Increase the speed to medium and mix until the gluten develops, about 3 minutes. To check if the gluten has developed, "pull a window" by taking a handful of the dough and stretching it apart. If you can stretch the dough so thin that you can see through it (like a window) without it ripping, then you're good to go.

3. Form the dough into a ball, place it in the oiled bowl, cover with plastic wrap, and proof in a warm place for 1 hour.

4. Turn the dough over, press it down, fold it in, and flip it over. Continue to proof for another 30 minutes.

5. Preheat the oven to 350°F. Line a sheet pan with parchment paper, dust lightly with cornmeal, and set aside.

6. Transfer the dough to a floured, clean work surface and pat down the dough until it's about ½ inch thick.

7. Using a ring mold, cut out 12 to 15 circles of dough and set aside.

8. In a large sauté pan over medium heat, warm the oil and the remaining 2 tablespoons of butter. Carefully place the dough circles into the sauté pan and cook until browned, 3 to 4 minutes. Turn and continue to cook until browned, another 2 minutes.

   PRO TIP: Be careful not to deflate the dough when handling it so that you can ensure lots of those signature "nooks and crannies."

9. Transfer the muffins to the prepared sheet pan and bake for 5 to 7 minutes, or until golden brown.

10. Store the English muffins, wrapped in plastic wrap, in the freezer for up to 2 months.

Serving Tip: Toast these and serve with butter and jam or use them to make eggs Benedict or an egg and sausage sandwich.

Technique Tip: The sponge step is a sort of pre-mix that helps add flavor and texture and helps with the chemistry of your dough.

Bagels

Prep time: 2 days • **Cook time:** 10 to 12 minutes

You won't find a better bagel than one made in New York City. Rumor is it's because of the water (the same theory is attached to NYC pizza dough). But I know of another reason our bagels are ranked so highly: They are boiled first, *then* baked. That's what gives you that crispy shell and fluffy, chewy interior. If you can't make it to New York any time soon, this recipe will give you that authentic taste and texture at home. • *Yield: 8 bagels*

For the dough

Oil, for greasing the bowl
600 grams bread flour
28 grams malt syrup
   or 10 grams diastatic
   malt powder
15 grams salt
4½ grams instant dry yeast
350 milliliters water

For the poaching liquid

1 tablespoon baking soda
1 tablespoon malt syrup

Optional toppings

Sesame seeds
Poppy seeds
Dehydrated onion
Dehydrated garlic
Flaky sea salt

Day 1

1. Oil a large bowl and set aside.

2. In the bowl of a stand mixer fitted with the hook attachment, combine the bread flour, malt syrup, salt, yeast, and water and mix on low speed until incorporated, about 5 minutes. Increase the speed to high and continue to mix until the dough is smooth and not sticky, about 2 minutes.

3. Place the dough in the oiled bowl, cover with plastic wrap, and proof in a warm place until it doubles in size, about 1 hour.

4. Punch down the dough and let rest for 10 minutes.

5. Divide the dough into balls weighing about 120 grams each. Roll each ball into a log. Wrap each dough log around your hand to make a ring and use your palm to roll over the ends that meet in order to fuse them together.

6. Place each dough ring on a sheet pan lined with parchment paper, cover with plastic wrap, and refrigerate overnight.

Day 2

1. Preheat the oven to 350°F.

2. Fill a large stockpot with water. Stir in the baking soda and malt syrup and bring to a boil over high heat. Carefully drop in 2 or 3 bagels, taking care not to overcrowd the pot, and boil on each side for 40 to 60 seconds. Remove from the water and place on the sheet pan.

3. Sprinkle the bagels with the toppings of your choice.

4. Bake for 10 to 12 minutes, or until golden brown. Let cool on a wire rack.

5. Store bagels in an airtight container at room temperature for up to 2 days or freeze in zip-top plastic bags for up to 1 month.

Technique Tip: If you don't have a stand mixer, mix the ingredients in a large bowl until combined. Turn out the dough mixture onto a lightly floured work surface and knead for 10 minutes.

Pretzel Rolls

Prep time: 2 hours • **Cook time:** 15 to 17 minutes

I can clearly remember the first time I had a pretzel roll. I bought a package of frozen rolls, popped them in the oven, cracked one open, and slathered on some butter. I was hooked. I believe I ate four of them for my dinner that night. Since then, I've learned to make my own and I think I love them even more. Cut them in half and use them for sandwiches or eat them plain with a slab of butter. • *Yield: 10 rolls*

500 grams all-purpose flour,
   plus more for dusting
300 milliliters water, plus
   1 liter at room temperature
42 grams melted
   unsalted butter
7 grams instant dry yeast
2 teaspoons salt
54 grams baking soda
Coarse sea salt, for topping

1. In the bowl of a stand mixer fitted with the hook attachment, combine the flour, 300 milliliters of water, butter, yeast, and salt and mix on low speed until everything is combined, about 2 minutes.

2. Increase the speed to medium and mix until the dough is smooth and elastic, 2 to 3 minutes.

3. Transfer the dough to a clean, floured work surface. Knead the dough a few times and form it into a ball.

4. Transfer the dough back into the stand mixer bowl. Cover with plastic wrap, place in a warm area, and proof until doubled in size, about 1 hour.

5. Line a sheet pan with parchment paper.

6. Punch down the dough and knead it again for about 1 minute.

7. Divide the dough into 10 equal pieces, about 85 grams each. Flour your hand a bit and create a "cage" over the piece of dough. Using very little pressure, roll the dough around, letting your palm shape the dough into a smooth ball, and place it on the prepared sheet pan. Repeat with the rest of the dough pieces.

8. Proof the dough balls in a warm place until they appear a bit puffier and they jiggle a bit when you shake the tray, about 20 minutes.

9. Preheat the oven to 425°F. Line 2 sheet pans with parchment paper.

10. In a large stockpot, mix together the baking soda and 1 liter of water and bring to a boil.

11. Gently place 2 or 3 dough balls into the boiling water. Cook for about 30 seconds, then flip the dough over and cook for another 30 seconds. Transfer to a wire rack to dry. (It is important for the dough to be dry before baking to develop that nice brown crust.) Repeat with the rest of the dough balls.

12. Transfer the dry dough balls to the prepared sheet pans. Using a sharp paring knife, score a cross on top of each ball of dough and sprinkle with coarse sea salt.

13. Bake for 15 to 17 minutes, or until golden brown. Let cool on a wire rack.

14. Store the rolls in a zip-top plastic bag at room temperature for up to 5 days or in the freezer for up to 1 month.

Technique Tip: If you don't have a stand mixer, mix the ingredients in a large bowl until combined. Turn out the dough mixture onto a lightly floured work surface and knead for 10 minutes.

Serving Tip: These are best served right out of the oven, but you can freeze them in a zip-top bag for up to 4 weeks.

Japanese Milk Bread

Prep time: 2 hours　•　**Cook time:** 35 to 40 minutes

Japanese milk bread has a soft, super fluffy texture and a little bit of sweetness, which makes it one of my favorite go-to breads when I'm craving something slightly sweet. Cut it into slices and use for cinnamon-sugar toast or an elevated peanut butter and jelly sandwich.　•　*Yield: 2 (9-by-5-inch) loaves or 16 rolls*

Starter

120 milliliters whole milk
45 grams bread flour
120 milliliters water

Dough

Oil, for greasing the bowl
650 grams bread flour
120 grams granulated sugar
14 grams instant dry yeast
4 tablespoons dried
　milk powder
2 teaspoons salt
227 milliliters warmed milk
2 large eggs, at
　room temperature
120 grams unsalted butter, at
　room temperature, plus more
　for greasing the pans
Heavy cream, for brushing

To make the starter

In a medium saucepan over medium heat, mix together the milk, bread flour, and water. Cook, stirring constantly to keep the mixture from sticking, until the mixture has reached a thick consistency (like mashed potatoes). Transfer the mixture to a medium bowl and cover with plastic wrap, letting the plastic wrap touch the dough to prevent a skin from forming. Set it aside and let it to come to room temperature.

To make the dough and bake the bread

1. Oil a large bowl.

2. In the bowl of a stand mixer fitted with the paddle attachment, combine the bread flour, sugar, yeast, milk powder, and salt and mix on low speed for just a few seconds. Add the cooled starter, milk, and eggs and mix on low speed for about 5 minutes.

3. Add the butter and continue to mix until it is fully incorporated, 3 to 4 minutes. Increase the speed to medium and continue to mix for an additional 5 minutes, or until the dough begins to pull away from the sides of the bowl.

4. Place the dough in the oiled bowl, cover with a kitchen towel, and proof until the dough has doubled in size, about 1 hour.

5. Grease 2 (9-by-5-inch) loaf pans or, for rolls, 2 (8- to 10-inch) cake pans with butter and line them with parchment paper.

6. Divide the dough in half. Be sure to cover any dough that you're not working with to prevent a skin from forming.

7. To make loaves: Divide each half of the dough into 4 pieces. Using your hands, roll the 8 pieces of dough into balls. With a rolling pin, roll out each ball of dough into an 8-by-5-inch rectangle. Fold in each side of one dough rectangle about 1 inch. Using your hands, roll the folded dough, starting from a short side of the rectangle, to create a log. Place the log crosswise in a prepared loaf pan, seam-side down. Repeat this with the remaining pieces of dough, fitting 4 logs in each loaf pan. Proceed to step 9.

8. To make rolls: Divide each half of the dough into 8 pieces. Using your hands, shape the 16 pieces of dough into balls. Place 8 dough balls into each prepared cake pan.

9. Cover the pans with plastic wrap and proof until the dough is doubled in size, about 30 minutes.

10. Preheat the oven to 350°F.

11. Brush the loaves or rolls with heavy cream and bake for 35 to 40 minutes, or until the tops are evenly browned. Let the bread rest in the pan for about 5 minutes before removing and cooling completely on a wire rack.

12. Store bread or rolls in an airtight container at room temperature for up to 5 days or in the freezer wrapped tightly in plastic wrap for up to 2 months.

Serving Tip: Always use a serrated knife when cutting bread. This allows you to cut through the bread without flattening it, which is especially important for breads like this that are very soft and delicate.

Technique Tip: A *starter* is a mixture of flour, yeast (or some kind of culture), and water. Also known as a *pre-ferment*, it adds an additional depth of flavor and helps create a fluffier dough. This process of cooking the starter on the stove top before using it in the dough is called *tangzhong*, which means "water roux."

Levain Starter

Prep time: 5 days

You can either purchase a starter, take some from a friend who has already started theirs, or start your very own with just a few ingredients and simple steps. This kind of starter uses the wild yeasts in the air instead of a purchased yeast, and it will add unique flavors to the bread. Be mindful to check on your starter regularly, because just like a pet, it requires feeding and attention. It's worth your time, though, as most delicious breads start with a great starter. The amounts of flour and water in this recipe are for beginning the starter. It will need to be fed for at least 3 days before it is ready to use, so be sure to have plenty of flour on hand. When the starter is ready to use in recipes, try making Sourdough (page 40) to test it out.

500 grams all-purpose
   flour, divided
500 milliliters lukewarm
   water, divided

Day 1

1. In a medium container, mix together 250 grams of flour and 250 milliliters of water until they are fully combined and there are no pockets of dry flour left.

2. Cover the container loosely with a lid, or if you're using plastic wrap, poke a few holes in it. This will allow any gases to escape while the yeast forms.

3. Let the mixture sit in a warm place for 24 hours. (I like to put mine on top of the refrigerator.)

Day 2

1. After 24 hours, you should begin seeing some growth and bubbling.

2. In another container, mix together the remaining 250 grams of flour and the remaining 250 grams of lukewarm water until fully combined. Add 150 grams of the initial starter to this new mixture and discard the rest. This is called "feeding" the starter.

3. Cover the new mixture loosely and let sit in a warm place.

Maintaining the starter

1. From this point, you will repeat the instructions for
    Day 2 every 12 hours, for 6 feedings (3 days). At each
    feeding, you should notice more and more activity, signal-
    ing more yeast development and the makings of a healthy
    starter. At that point, your starter will be strong enough
    to begin using in recipes. After two weeks of twice-daily
    feedings, it will be at optimal strength.

2. The starter can last indefinitely if you keep feeding
    it. If you're not using it every day, you can place it in
    the refrigerator and feed it only once a week, using
    125 milliliters of water and 125 grams of flour. If you
    want to store it without feeding it, freeze it. To use,
    defrost it in the refrigerator and resume the feedings.
    If you want to increase the amount, feed it 125 grams of
    flour and 125 milliliters of water until you reach your
    desired quantity.

Sourdough

Prep time: 4 to 6 hours • **Cook time:** 1 hour

Crispy, chewy, and with that signature sour taste the world loves so much, sourdough is the kind of bread that goes with everything. I particularly like it for soups and sandwiches. Although some hardcore bread bakers think it takes a lifetime to master sourdough, a little practice will actually result in a delicious and highly satisfying loaf. • *Yield: 1 boule*

100 grams Levain Starter
   (page 38)
300 milliliters warm water
500 grams bread flour
10 grams sea salt
Oil, for greasing the bowl

1. In a large bowl, mix together the starter and water. Add the flour and salt and, using your hands, mix together until there are no dry pockets. Let the dough rest for 30 minutes.

2. Remove the dough from the bowl and shape into a ball. Lightly oil the bowl. Place the dough back into the bowl, cover loosely with a kitchen towel, and proof until the dough has doubled in size, 2 to 4 hours.

3. During this process, to help increase its total volume, the dough can be folded and stretched. Take one side of the dough, stretch it out, and fold it back into the dough. Do this once or twice during the proofing process, making sure to let it proof for at least 1 hour between stretching.

4. Shape the proofed dough into a large ball or boule by placing it on a clean work surface, then taking 1 edge of dough and pulling it toward the center. Continue working your way around the dough until you form a nice tight ball. (Dust your hands with a little flour if the dough is too sticky, but don't flour the work surface or the dough will slide around too much. The goal is to create tension in the dough to make a tight ball.)

5. Line a Dutch oven with parchment paper. Place the formed boule in the Dutch oven, seam-side down. Let the dough proof until it has puffed up, about 1 hour.

6. Preheat the oven to 450°F.

7. Using a sharp paring knife or a lame, score the top of the boule.

8. Place the lid on the Dutch oven. Lower the oven temperature to 400°F and bake for 20 minutes. Remove the lid and bake for an additional 40 minutes, or until your bread is deep golden or dark brown and the internal temperature is at least 208°F.

9. Remove the bread from the Dutch oven and let cool completely on a wire rack, about 1 hour.

Troubleshooting Tip: Make sure you let the bread cool completely. It can be tempting to cut slices of warm bread, but if you give in to that impulse, you'll see that the bread will be harder to cut and the interior will be overly moist and gummy.

Chapter Three

Pastries and Desserts

Crème Brûlée, page 69 (left)

Tips of the Trade

At this point, you're pretty comfortable in the kitchen and you have the basic baking guidelines under your belt, but here are some tips about pastry and desserts that you'll find useful for the recipes in this chapter.

Burning the Eggs

I know this one sounds funny. Here's what I mean: People will often mix their eggs and sugar together at some point in the baking process and then set them aside, thinking they're prepping and saving time. The problem with this is that sugar is hydroscopic, meaning it pulls moisture out of whatever it comes into contact with. Leaving sugar mixed with eggs causes them to dry out and create hard bits in your batter. That process is referred to as "burning your eggs."

Chilling the Dough

If you're like me, your hands may run a little on the warmer side, and this makes your life that much harder when handling delicate doughs (or, even worse, chocolate). No worries! When you feel your dough starting to get too soft or you notice the fat (butter or shortening) is starting to melt out, put the dough in the refrigerator for 15 minutes or so and continue working.

Preheating the Oven

This is pretty fundamental, but I've been guilty of this myself: I forget to preheat the oven and I throw my bakes into it before it's heated to the proper temperature. It's actually very important to preheat your oven to allow your bake to get that initial burst of heat when it goes into the oven.

Adding Too Much Flour

I mentioned this briefly in the previous chapter, too, but it's worth repeating. You never want to flour your working surface too much because it will inadvertently add more flour to the recipe. As we should all know by now, baking is a precise science with exact measurements. If you use more than a light dusting, you run the risk of your dough or batter becoming too dry and tough.

Using the Middle Rack

How many times have you put your tray too close to the top or the bottom, resulting in unevenly browned or burnt goods? I always advise to use the middle rack; this is the best way to ensure that your baked goods are getting sufficient heat from above and below. For this reason, it's best to bake one pan at a time to ensure consistently baked treats, or adjust your racks to all fit as closely to the center of the oven as possible.

Pastry Cream

Prep time: 15 minutes, plus time to cool • **Cook time:** 10 minutes

Pastry cream is a staple in baking and dessert making. It's the perfect filling for so many confections, including Éclairs (page 54) and Banana Cream Tart (page 90), to name just a couple. It's amazingly flexible and can be infused with so many wonderful flavors, from chocolate and coffee to orange and raspberry. Get ready for a workout, though, because this recipe requires some strong whisking skills. • *Yield: 540 grams*

474 milliliters whole milk

125 grams granulated
   sugar, divided

Seeds of ½ split vanilla bean
   or 1 teaspoon vanilla extract
   or paste

1 large egg

2 large egg yolks

50 grams cornstarch

25 grams unsalted butter

1. Line a sheet pan with plastic wrap, leaving enough extra over the edges to fold back and cover the pastry cream.

2. In a medium saucepan over high heat, mix together the milk, 62.5 grams of sugar, and the vanilla and bring to a boil, stirring frequently to make sure the milk doesn't burn and stick to the pot.

3. In a medium bowl, whisk together the egg, egg yolks, the remaining 62.5 grams of sugar, and the cornstarch until smooth.

4. Temper the egg mixture by adding about one-third of the hot milk to the egg mixture and whisking to combine.

5. Add the tempered egg mixture to the saucepan and bring to a boil, whisking vigorously for 2 full minutes.

   PRO TIP: This step is crucial for developing the thickness of the pastry cream. You must cook the pastry cream mixture for a full 2 minutes once everything is combined in order to kill the alpha-amylase enzymes that can cause the pastry cream to separate once it's cooled.

6. Add the butter and stir until it's incorporated into the mixture.

7. Pour the pastry cream onto the plastic-lined sheet pan and carefully fold the plastic wrap over the pastry cream, making sure the plastic wrap is touching the surface of the pastry cream. This will prevent a skin from forming.

8. Place the sheet pan in the refrigerator to cool completely.

9. When ready to use, you can add additional flavoring, such as melted chocolate or extracts. Spoon the pastry cream into the bowl of a stand mixer fitted with the paddle attachment and mix with the flavoring for 1 to 2 minutes until fully incorporated and the pastry cream loosens up a bit.

10. The pastry cream can be stored, with plastic wrap touching the surface, in an airtight container in the refrigerator for up to 4 days.

Technique Tip: You can make a crème légère by mixing freshly whipped cream with the pastry cream. This is best used as a lighter cake filling or as a filling for éclairs.

Puff Pastry

Prep time: 2 hours

This is a classic dough that every good baker should know. It can be used for sweet or savory dishes, making it super versatile depending on the fillings you use. Like most laminated doughs, puff pastry is known for its flaky and buttery layers. Use it to make Cheese Straws (page 21) or a classic Napoleon (page 66). • *Yield: 675 grams*

250 grams all-purpose flour

1 teaspoon salt

40 grams softened
  unsalted butter

125 milliliters cold water, plus
  more as needed

250 grams cold
  unsalted butter

1. In the bowl of a stand mixer fitted with the paddle attachment, combine the flour and salt and mix briefly. Add the softened butter and mix to combine.

2. With the mixer on low, add the cold water slowly until the ingredients are just combined, being mindful to stop when the dough appears shaggy—not completely wet. You may use more or less of the water than is called for.

3. Shape the dough into a square, wrap tightly in plastic wrap, and refrigerate for at least 30 minutes.

4. Using a rolling pin, soften the cold butter by pounding it into a 6-by-6-inch square. Wrap the butter block in plastic and set aside.

5. Roll out the chilled dough into a 6-by-6-inch square, the same size as the butter block. Carefully roll out just the corners of the dough to form flaps (these should be big enough to meet in the center when folded). The dough will naturally be a little thinner on the flaps, leaving a little hump in the center of the dough.

6. Place the butter block in the center of the dough, and fold the flaps over the butter.

7. Roll out the dough into a long rectangle about ⅜ inch thick.

8. Now you're going to make what is called a "turn." Fold the rectangle in thirds by bringing one short side toward the center and making one fold, then taking the opposite side and placing it on top. Turn the dough 90 degrees so that it resembles a book with the opening on the right side.

9. Mark the top right corner by gently pressing your finger into the dough. This will help you keep track of how many turns you've made. Place the dough in the refrigerator for at least 30 minutes.

10. Repeat steps 7 through 9 for a total of 6 turns. Make sure to mark each turn with your fingers (1 finger for the first turn, 2 fingers for the second turn, etc.). Also remember to always start rolling with the folded dough's opening on the right-hand side.

11. Use the puff pastry right away or store it, wrapped tightly in plastic wrap, in the refrigerator for up to 3 days or for up to 1 month in the freezer.

Technique Tips:

- *Softening butter.* I like to soften butter by wrapping it in plastic wrap and pressing it between my fingers until it's really soft.
- *Chilling dough.* If at any point you feel the dough becoming too warm and soft, place it back in the refrigerator immediately for about 10 minutes.
- *Relaxing dough.* If you notice that the dough springs back and shrinks while you're rolling it out, that means the gluten needs to relax. Place it back in the refrigerator for about 10 minutes.

Cream Puffs

Prep time: 45 minutes　·　**Cook time:** 35 minutes

Pâte à choux is a versatile dough that can be used in many recipes and is the base for cream puffs, one of the simplest—and most impressive—desserts you can whip up in a relatively short period of time. You probably already have all the ingredients in your kitchen.　·　*Yield: About 40 cream puffs*

For the pâte à choux

125 grams unsalted butter, cut into small cubes, at room temperature

33 grams granulated sugar

2 grams salt

235 milliliters water

175 grams bread flour or all-purpose flour

5 or 6 large eggs, plus 1 egg, beaten, for egg wash

For the filling

1 recipe Pastry Cream (page 46)

To make the pâte à choux

1. In a large saucepan over high heat, mix together the butter, sugar, salt, and water and bring to a boil.

2. Lower the heat to medium and immediately add the flour, stirring vigorously with a wooden spoon, until the dough forms a ball and pulls away from the side of the pot. Continue to stir to dry out the dough, another 1 to 2 minutes.

   PRO TIP: Using a wooden spoon will keep the temperature of the dough even as you stir the batter.

3. Transfer the dough to the bowl of a stand mixer fitted with the paddle attachment and mix on medium-low speed until you no longer see large amounts of steam and the dough has cooled down.

4. Crack 5 eggs in a separate bowl. With the mixer on low, add one egg at a time, letting each one mix completely into the dough before adding the next one, until the dough is firm and smooth. Test by dipping the paddle into the dough: If the dough falls back onto itself, forming a ribbon, it's ready. If necessary, mix in another egg until the dough reaches the proper consistency.

5. Preheat the oven to 500°F. Line a sheet pan with parchment paper.

6. Spoon some of the dough into a pastry bag fitted with an Ateco #805 round tip. Pipe the dough in 1-inch rounds on the prepared sheet pan. Brush the piped dough with the egg wash.

7. Place the sheet pan in the oven, turn the oven off, and bake for 15 minutes. Turn the oven back on to 350°F degrees and continue to bake until the puffs are golden brown, about 20 minutes. Let cool on a wire rack.

To fill the cream puffs

Use an Ateco #821 star tip to make a hole in the bottom of each puff. Spoon the pastry cream into a pastry bag fitted with an Ateco #801 tip and pipe the cream into the bottom of each puff. You'll know when there is enough filling when the cream puff feels heavy.

Serving Tip: These can also be filled with whipped cream or crème légère. Or, for an extra special treat, you can slice these in half and fill with a small scoop of your favorite ice cream. Drizzle with chocolate or caramel sauce and serve as lovely plated profiteroles.

Technique Tip: It's important to add the flour to the butter mixture right away to make sure the liquid doesn't start to evaporate and change the ratio of liquid to flour in the recipe.

Troubleshooting Tip: If you've added too many eggs and your dough is too soft, DO NOT add more flour. Make half of the recipe again without eggs and add that to your runny choux dough. It will firm up and you'll be good to go. Another way to tell if the dough has enough eggs is to run your finger or the end of a spoon across the batter. It should leave a channel that slowly fills itself in.

Lady Fingers

Prep time: 20 minutes • **Cook time:** 5 to 7 minutes

Lady fingers are the unsung heroes of desserts. They are lovely on their own with a cup of tea or coffee, but they really shine in wonderful treats like Tiramisu (page 53). You can even make a simple strawberry shortcake with lady fingers as the base. Once you realize how quickly these can be made, you'll never want to buy them from the grocery store again. • *Yield: 20 to 24 lady fingers*

5 large eggs, separated

125 grams confectioners' sugar, plus more for dusting

½ teaspoon vanilla extract

Pinch salt

125 grams cake flour, sifted

1. Preheat the oven to 350°F. Line a sheet pan with parchment paper.

   PRO TIP: Before lining the sheet pan, fold the parchment paper in half lengthwise. This will give you a guide to see how long your lady fingers should be.

2. In the bowl of a stand mixer fitted with the whisk attachment, whisk the egg whites, confectioners' sugar, vanilla extract, and salt on low speed, gradually increasing the speed to medium-high, until the mixture reaches stiff peaks. Set aside.

3. In a medium bowl, whisk the egg yolks to break and loosen them before gently folding them into the egg white mixture.

4. Fold in the cake flour, being very careful not to deflate the mixture.

5. Fill a pastry bag fitted with an Ateco #805 round tip with the batter and pipe 6-inch-long lady fingers on the parchment paper.

6. Dust the lady fingers with confectioners' sugar and bake for 5 to 7 minutes, or until they are lightly browned and spring back when pressed.

Technique Tips:

- *Salt.* Adding a pinch of salt to the eggs and confectioners' sugar helps stabilize the whites as they are beaten.
- *Whisking egg whites.* Always start on a low speed and gradually work your way up to a higher speed.

Tiramisu

Prep time: 1 hour 35 minutes, plus 5 hours to set • Cook time: 10 minutes

Whenever I go out to a restaurant, if I see it on the menu, no matter how full I already am, I have to order the tiramisu. It's my all-time favorite dessert, and once I started making it myself, it became the dessert everyone asked me to bring to parties. With beautiful creamy layers and that zing of espresso, I suspect this will quickly become one of your favorites, too. • *Yield: 1 (9-by-11-inch) tiramisu*

6 large egg yolks

160 milliliters whole milk

156 grams granulated sugar

200 milliliters heavy cream

½ teaspoon vanilla extract

453 grams mascarpone cheese

1 teaspoon instant espresso

2 tablespoons rum

60 milliliters water

1 recipe Lady Fingers (page 52)

1 teaspoon unsweetened
  cocoa powder

1. In a medium saucepan over medium heat, whisk together the egg yolks, milk, and sugar and cook, stirring constantly, until it comes to a boil. Boil for 1 minute and remove from the heat. Transfer the mixture to a bowl, cover with plastic wrap so that it's touching the mixture, and place it in the refrigerator to cool for at least 1 hour.

2. In the bowl of a stand mixer fitted with the whisk attachment, whip the heavy cream until it reaches stiff peaks. In a separate bowl, mix together the cooled egg mixture, the vanilla, and mascarpone cheese until smooth. Gently fold the whipped cream into the cooled egg mixture.

3. In a medium bowl, mix together the instant espresso, rum, and water. Dip the lady fingers into the espresso mixture and arrange as many as will fit in the bottom of a 9-by-11-inch pan or trifle bowl.

4. Spread about one-third of the cream mixture over the lady fingers. Repeat with the remaining cream mixture and lady fingers, making sure to end with the cream mixture.

5. Dust the cocoa powder over the top. Cover the pan with plastic wrap and refrigerate for a minimum of 5 hours before serving.

6. Store tiramisu covered in plastic wrap in the refrigerator for up to 48 hours.

Technique Tip: I like to make this the night before I plan to serve it, which gives the flavors the perfect amount of time to meld.

Éclairs

Prep time: 15 minutes * Cook time: 35 to 40 minutes

I was happily surprised when I discovered that making éclairs was a lot simpler than I initially thought. Like Cream Puffs (page 50), all you need to do is make the pâte à choux and pipe it into the classic éclair shape. Decide on a filling and you're good to go. A truly decadent dessert, éclairs are easily one of my favorites, and I hope they become one of yours, as well. * *Yield: 20 to 25 (4-inch) éclairs*

For the éclairs

1 recipe pâte à choux
  (see page 50)
1 large egg, beaten, for
  egg wash

For the filling

150 milliliters heavy cream
½ recipe Pastry Cream
  (page 46)

For the chocolate glaze

112 grams semisweet
  chocolate
113 milliliters heavy cream

To make the éclairs

1. Preheat the oven to 500°F. Line a sheet pan with parchment paper.

   PRO TIP: Mark 4-inch lines with a pencil on the parchment paper, then flip it over to line the pan. When you pipe the dough, you'll be able to follow the marks and make consistently sized éclairs.

2. Fill a pastry bag fitted with an Ateco #829 star tip with the pâte à choux, being careful not to overfill the bag, which will allow for better control while you're piping.

3. Pipe the dough evenly onto the prepared sheet pan in straight lines about 4 inches long. Make sure to leave room between éclairs, as they will puff up in the oven.

4. Brush the tops of the éclairs with the egg wash. (If you used a round tip to pipe the dough, drag a fork down the length of the dough. This will create "cracks" that will let steam escape while baking and allow your dough to puff.)

5. Place the sheet pan in the oven and turn off the heat immediately. Bake for 15 minutes. Turn the oven on to 350°F and continue to bake for 25 minutes, or until golden brown.

6. Let cool completely. Using a smaller star pastry tip, create two holes on the bottom of each éclair.

7. Unfilled éclairs can be stored in an airtight container for up to 3 days and frozen for up to 1 month. Defrost frozen éclairs in the refrigerator for about 30 to 40 minutes to prevent condensation and sogginess. Let defrost completely before filling.

To make the filling and fill the éclairs

1. In a stand mixer fitted with the whisk attachment, whip the cream until it reaches medium peaks. Create a crème légère by folding the whipped cream into the pastry cream.

2. Fill a pastry bag fitted with an Ateco #822 star tip with the crème légère and pipe it into the two holes you made in the éclairs. To make sure that you're getting enough filling into each éclair, give it a little shake. This will help spread the filling all the way to both ends. When the éclair is filled properly, it should have some weight to it.

To make the chocolate glaze and finish the éclairs

1. Place the chocolate in a medium bowl. In a double boiler over medium heat, warm the heavy cream until bubbles start to form around the edges. Pour it over the chocolate and let the mixture sit for about 2 minutes. Whisk the mixture, from the center outward, until well combined.

2. Dip the tops of the éclairs in the chocolate and serve.

Technique Tip: Crème légère is a mixture of pastry cream and whipped cream, which is a common filling for éclairs and is also used frequently in tarts and trifles.

Variation Tip: Lightly dust the éclairs with confectioners' sugar instead of using a glaze. If you are glazing, add small pieces of fruit on top, such as raspberries, or sprinkle the tops with shredded coconut.

Croquembouche

Prep time: 2 hours • **Cook time:** 8 to 10 minutes

This is one of the fanciest and most show-stopping desserts you can possibly make. Cream puffs are stacked into a pyramid, which is held together with caramelized sugar and decorated with strands of spun sugar. Not only is it a beautiful centerpiece for any table, but it's actually quite delicious! Literally translating to "crunch in the mouth," these delectable puffs come together to create a really special dessert that you should make at least once in your life. This croquembouche is built on a base of Pâte Sucrée (page 81), though you could use a croquembouche mold to build the cream puff tower, in which case you won't need the base. • *Yield: 1 croquembouche*

½ recipe Pâte Sucrée (page 81)

Flour, for dusting

400 grams granulated sugar, divided

1 recipe Cream Puffs (page 50)

1. Preheat the oven to 350°F. Line a sheet pan with parchment paper.

2. Roll out the pâte sucrée on a lightly floured work surface to about ¼ inch thick. Cut the dough into a 9-inch circle.

3. Bake for 8 to 10 minutes, or until golden brown. Set aside to cool. This will be the base for the croquembouche.

4. In a medium saucepan over medium-low heat, melt 100 grams of the sugar. As the sugar melts, add more to the pan and use a spoon to drag the sugar crystals into the melted sugar. Keep adding the sugar until it's all melted. Be mindful not to stir aggressively. Let the sugar melt on its own to limit any recrystallization. Place a candy thermometer into the saucepan and cook until the sugar reaches between 355°F and 360°F. The sugar should be golden brown. Immediately remove from the stove.

5. To build the croquembouche, dip one of the sides of the filled cream puffs in the caramelized sugar and place it on the edge of the base. Repeat until you have a ring of about 9 cream puffs for the base. Layer the remaining cream puffs in successive rings, decreasing by one cream puff per layer. If at any point the sugar becomes too hard, warm it up on the stove over low heat until it softens again.

6. Once all the cream puffs are used, dip a fork into the sugar and, with the sugar attached to it, wrap it around the croquembouche, creating sugar strands all around the outside.

7. Place the croquembouche in the refrigerator for 5 to 7 minutes, or until firm. Serve immediately.

Troubleshooting Tip: When creating a croquembouche, make sure you know the guest count and allow for two cream puffs per person. Then you will know how many cream puffs you need and how to best construct your croquembouche.

Paris-Brest

Prep time: 20 minutes · **Cook time:** 35 to 40 minutes

This French dessert was created as a tribute to the Paris-Brest bicycle race and resembles a bicycle wheel. It is one of the most popular desserts in France and is the type of fancy dessert that is deceptively easy to make. · *Yield: 1 (8-inch) Paris-Brest*

For the pastry

½ recipe pâte à choux
  (see page 50)
1 large egg, beaten, for
  egg wash
50 grams sliced almonds,
  soaked in water for
  10 minutes

For the filling

175 grams unsalted butter
100 grams hazelnut
  praline paste
300 grams Pastry Cream
  (page 46), cooled
Confectioners' sugar,
  for dusting

To make the pastry

1. Preheat the oven to 500°F.

2. Draw a 7-inch circle on a piece of parchment paper, flip it over, and line a sheet pan with it.

3. Fill a piping bag fitted with an Ateco #807 round tip with the pâte à choux and pipe a ring just outside of the circle you drew. Pipe another ring on the inside of the circle. The two rings should be touching.

4. Pipe a third ring on top of where the two rings meet.

5. Brush the entire ring with egg wash. Drain the almonds, pat them dry, and sprinkle them over the dough.

6. Place the sheet pan in the oven and turn off the heat. Bake for 15 minutes. Turn the oven back on and set the temperature to 350°F. Continue to bake for 20 to 25 minutes, or until the pastry is golden brown and the underside has small cracks. Let cool on a wire rack.

To make the filling

In the bowl of a stand mixer fitted with the paddle attachment, mix the butter and praline paste on medium speed, making sure to scrape down the sides of the bowl, until well combined, light, and fluffy. Add the cooled pastry cream and mix until well combined.

To assemble the Paris-Brest

1. Using a serrated knife, carefully cut the pastry ring in half horizontally.

2. Fill a pastry bag fitted with a star tip with the filling and pipe it onto the bottom half of the ring, using a circular motion to create a rope design. Be sure to pipe close to the outside edge, as part of the design of this dessert is to see the filling. Place the top half of the ring over the filling.

3. Dust with confectioners' sugar and serve.

Technique Tip: Soaking the almonds in water keeps them from burning while the pastry is baking.

Croissants

Prep time: 15 hours • Cook time: 15 to 20 minutes

My favorite pastry is a plain croissant. No jam, no butter, nothing extra—just a crispy, soft, delicate croissant and I'm instantly in my happy place. Not that this ever happens in my house (they don't last that long), but should you find your croissants have gone stale, make Almond Croissants (page 74) for something special. • *Yield: 12 croissants*

100 milliliters whole milk

8 grams instant dry yeast

190 milliliters water

500 grams bread flour, plus more for dusting

65 grams granulated sugar

20 grams softened butter, plus 230 grams cold unsalted butter

10 grams salt

1 large egg, beaten, for egg wash

1. Line a sheet pan with parchment paper.

2. In a medium bowl, combine the milk, yeast, and water. Let sit until the mixture bubbles up, about 2 minutes.

3. In the bowl of a stand mixer fitted with the paddle attachment, combine the flour, sugar, 20 grams of softened butter, salt, and the yeast mixture and mix on low to medium speed until the dough is well combined and smooth, 3 to 6 minutes. The dough will be sticky as there should not be a lot of gluten development.

4. Remove the dough from the bowl and, using your hands, form it into a ball and place it on the prepared sheet pan. Cover with plastic wrap and let proof in a warm place until it almost doubles in size, about 1 hour.

5. Roll out the dough on a lightly floured work surface into a 12-by-12-inch square and place it back on the sheet pan. Wrap the entire pan in plastic wrap and place it in the refrigerator for 1 hour to rest.

6. While the dough is resting, prepare the butter layer for the croissants. Place the remaining 230 grams of cold butter between two sheets of parchment paper. Using a rolling pin, shape the butter into a 6-by-12-inch rectangle and place it in the refrigerator.

7. Remove the dough from the refrigerator and place it on a lightly floured work surface. Place the rolled-out butter, which should be the same height as the dough, in the center of the dough. Fold the dough over the butter so that the two sides meet each other, creating a seam down the middle.

8. Using the rolling pin, press the dough and butter together a bit. This will help make the butter more pliable and able to stretch along with the dough. You now have three layers; dough, butter, and dough. The butter wrapped in dough is called a *pâton*.

9. Begin to roll out the dough into about a 30-by-8-inch rectangle. You will now perform what is known as a "book turn" or a double turn. Take the top edge of the dough and fold it down to the middle of the pâton and fold the bottom edge up, to have both edges meet in the middle. Now fold one half on top of the other, as if you were closing a book.

10. With the "spine" to the left, roll out the pâton once again to a 30-by-8-inch rectangle. Now you will perform a single turn. Fold the rectangle in thirds: Bring one end toward the center, making one fold, then take the other end and place it on top. Turn your dough 90 degrees so that it now resembles a book again, with the opening on the right side.

11. Roll out the dough into a 12-by-8-inch rectangle, place it on a parchment-lined sheet pan, and refrigerate for at least 1 hour, or overnight.

12. The next morning, remove the dough from the refrigerator. On a lightly floured surface, roll out the dough into an 18-by-8-inch rectangle. Using a knife, cut the dough in half lengthwise. Each strip should be 4 inches wide.

    PRO TIP: Do not drag your knife, as this will damage the layers. Instead, use a slicing motion.

13. Cut the strips crosswise to create 6 (4-by-6-inch) rectangles. Cut each rectangle diagonally to create two triangles. You should have 12 triangles.

continued →

14. To form the croissants, take a triangle and give it a little stretch to elongate it slightly. Using a sharp knife, cut a ½-inch slit in the middle of the wide side of the triangle. Starting at the cut side, use the palms of your hands to roll the dough, pressing outward to create that classic curved crescent shape. Place it on the sheet pan. Repeat with the rest of the triangles.

15. Brush each croissant with the egg wash. Cover the pan with aluminum foil, making sure that the foil does not touch the dough, and let it sit in a warm area until the dough rises and the croissants jiggle just a bit when you shake the sheet pan, 30 to 40 minutes.

16. Preheat the oven to 350°F.

17. Brush the croissants with the egg wash one more time and bake for 15 minutes. If they are browning unevenly, rotate the tray and bake for another 5 minutes, until evenly browned. Let cool on a wire rack.

18. Croissants are best served the same day they are made, but they can be stored in an airtight container at room temperature for up to 2 days.

Macarons

Prep time: 1 hour • **Cook time:** 10 to 12 minutes

Crunchy, sweet, and delicate, macarons are and always will be that quintessential French pastry that will wow you. These confectionary delights are incredibly versatile, coming in all kinds of flavors, shapes, and colors. Bonus: They're gluten-free! These macarons are made using the Italian meringue method of drizzling heated sugar syrup into whipped egg whites and continuing to whip until the mixture is stiff and satiny. Eat them as is or fill them with jam, ganache, or Swiss Meringue Buttercream (page 104). • *Yield: 25 to 30 (1½-inch) macarons*

125 grams almond flour

125 grams confectioners' sugar

125 grams granulated sugar

30 milliliters water

48 grams large egg whites

Pinch salt

Gel food coloring (optional)

1. Sift the almond flour and confectioners' sugar into a large bowl and mix until well combined.

2. To make the meringue, in a medium saucepan over medium heat, mix together the sugar and water. Cook without stirring to avoid forming sugar crystals, until the mixture starts to bubble. Use a pastry brush dipped in water to brush down any sugar that builds up on the sides of the pan. Place a candy thermometer in the pot.

3. Place the egg whites into the bowl of a stand mixer fitted with the whisk attachment. When the sugar syrup reaches 220°F, start whisking the eggs on low speed for 1 minute. Add the salt to help stabilize the eggs and raise the speed to medium. Whisk until the mixture forms medium peaks.

4. When the sugar syrup reaches between 235°F and 240°F (the soft ball stage), turn the mixer to high speed and add the sugar syrup, pouring it down the side of the bowl in a steady, even stream, which will prevent the syrup from pooling at the bottom of the bowl instead of dispersing throughout the meringue.

5. Continue whipping the meringue until the bowl is warm to the touch, 3 to 5 minutes. You now have Italian meringue.

6. Using a rubber spatula, fold the meringue into the almond flour mixture, one-third at a time to avoid over-mixing. This process is called *macaronage*. When the meringue has been completely mixed in, let the batter drop off the spatula. It should be loose enough that the

continued →

batter folds into a ribbon. Add gel food coloring (if using; see Technique Tip) and mix to combine. Cover the bowl with plastic wrap and set aside.

7. Draw 1-inch circles on a piece of parchment paper, flip it over, and line a sheet pan with it.

8. Fill a pastry bag fitted with an Ateco #804 round tip with the batter and pipe it onto the parchment paper, using the circles you drew as a guide. Holding the sheet pan firmly with both hands, bang the pan on a hard surface to release any air bubbles that may have formed inside the macarons. You can also use a toothpick to pop any visible bubbles on the surface.

9. Let the macarons sit and "dry" for about 30 minutes. This creates a skin on the top that traps the air when baking and pushes it outward, creating the signature "foot" along the edge of each macaron. Preheat the oven to 350°F.

10. Bake for 10 to 12 minutes, or until they just begin to lightly brown on the edges.

11. Let cool completely. Add your choice of fillings.

12. The macarons can be stored in an airtight container in one layer at room temperature for up to 1 day or in the refrigerator for up to 3 days.

Technique Tips:

- *Coloring the batter.* When using gel food coloring, a little bit can go a long way. Start with a small amount and add more slowly, until you reach the desired color.
- *Silicone mats.* Some silicone baking mats come printed with circles that you can use to pipe consistently sized macarons every time.

Upgrade Tip: Adding colors and/or flavors to macarons can really enhance them and make them special. Try matching the colors to the flavors.

- Pink macarons: Raspberry buttercream filling (you can also place a fresh raspberry in the middle and pipe the buttercream around it)
- Green macarons: Pistachio buttercream filling (you can roll the edges of the macarons in crushed pistachios)
- Yellow macarons: Lemon buttercream filling
- Brown macarons: Nutella buttercream filling

Napoleon

Prep time: 15 minutes　•　**Cook time:** 20 to 25 minutes

Also called *mille-feuille*, napoleons have to be one of the fanciest desserts around. Consisting of layers of crispy puff pastry and pastry cream and drizzled with glaze, these are very common in French-style bakeries. • *Yield: 1 (6-by-15-inch) napoleon*

For the puff pastry

Flour, for dusting

300 grams Puff Pastry
　(page 48)

Light corn syrup, for brushing

For the filling

100 milliliters heavy cream

500 grams Pastry Cream
　(page 46)

25 milliliters Grand Marnier

For the icing

150 grams confectioners' sugar

3 to 4 tablespoons milk
　or water

For the chocolate glaze

112 grams
　semisweet chocolate

113 milliliters heavy cream

To prepare the puff pastry

1. Preheat the oven to 350°F. Line a sheet pan with parchment paper.

2. On a lightly floured work surface, roll out the puff pastry into a rectangle about 15 by 18 inches wide and about ⅛ inch thick.

3. Place the dough onto the prepared sheet pan and dock the dough with a fork. Place another piece of parchment paper on top of the dough and another sheet pan on top of the parchment paper, creating a sandwich. This will ensure that the dough does not puff too much and remains flat.

4. Bake until the puff pastry is just starting to brown, 15 to 20 minutes. Brush the puff pastry with corn syrup and continue to bake, uncovered, for 5 more minutes.

5. Immediately cut the puff pastry into 3 (6-inch-wide) strips. Set aside.

6. The pastry strips can be made ahead of time and stored in an airtight container at room temperature for up to 2 days.

To make the filling

In the bowl of a stand mixer fitted with the whisk attachment, whip the heavy cream to stiff peaks. In another bowl, combine the pastry cream and Grand Marnier, then fold in the whipped cream in small amounts at a time so as not to deflate it. Watch to be sure the filling is thick enough to hold up the pastry layers. You may not use all the whipped cream.

To make the icing

In a small bowl, whisk together the confectioners' sugar and the water or milk until you have a thick yet spreadable texture.

To make the chocolate glaze

Place the chocolate in a medium bowl. In a double boiler over medium heat, warm the heavy cream until bubbles start to form around the edges. Pour it over the chocolate and let sit for about 2 minutes. Whisk the mixture from the center, outwards, until well combined. Let cool and transfer to a piping bag fitted with an Ateco #800 round tip.

To assemble the napoleon

1. Place one strip of puff pastry on a serving plate. Spoon or pipe half of the filling over the puff pastry. Add another layer of puff pastry and spread the remaining filling over it. Top with the last strip of puff pastry.

2. Spread the top of the napoleon with the icing. Before it sets, pipe thin chocolate lines lengthwise over the icing. Drag a paring knife across the lines of icing to create a beautiful design.

3. To serve, gently cut the napoleon into slices with a serrated knife, using a sawing motion so that the filling doesn't come out the sides.

Chocolate Soufflé

Prep time: 15 minutes　•　**Cook time:** 12 to 15 minutes

Soufflés have a reputation for being fussy and intimidating, but I'm here to tell you that's really not true. The key is to be gentle and not overmix. Once you master that, your soufflés will rise up and be beautiful.　•　*Yield: 4 (4-inch) soufflés*

60 grams unsalted butter, plus more for greasing the ramekins

40 grams granulated sugar, plus more for coating the ramekins

115 grams bittersweet chocolate

3 large eggs, separated

¼ teaspoon cream of tartar

Pinch salt

½ teaspoon raspberry, mint, or orange extract (optional)

Confectioners' sugar, for dusting (optional)

Whipped cream (optional)

1. Preheat the oven to 375°F. Heavily butter and sugar four (4-inch) ramekins.

2. In a large double boiler over medium heat, melt the chocolate and butter. Let cool and mix in the egg yolks. Set aside.

3. In the bowl of a stand mixer fitted with the whisk attachment, whip the egg whites, sugar, cream of tartar, and salt to stiff peaks. Add the flavored extract (if using) and whisk to combine.

4. Gently fold the whipped egg whites into the chocolate, being careful not to deflate the meringue.

5. Divide the mixture among the ramekins.

6. Bake for 12 to 15 minutes, or until the soufflés rise about 2 inches. Do not open the oven while they're baking.

7. Once slightly cooled, sprinkle the soufflés with confectioners' sugar or a dollop of whipped cream (if using) and serve immediately.

Technique Tip: Make sure the edges of the ramekins are clean of any batter. This will allow the soufflé to rise unimpeded.

Crème Brûlée

Prep time: 4 hours 15 minutes • **Cook time:** 35 to 40 minutes

Crème brûlée is a wonderful, creamy dessert with just the right amount of sweetness, though what really sets it apart is the crunchy burnt sugar layer on the top. There are few things more satisfying than tapping the sugar with a spoon and breaking through to the luscious custard inside. Divine. ⁎ *Yield: 4 (5-inch) crèmes brûlées*

500 milliliters heavy cream

70 grams granulated sugar, divided, plus more for topping

Pinch salt

1 vanilla bean, split and scraped, or 1½ teaspoons vanilla extract or paste

6 large egg yolks

1. Preheat the oven to 325°F.

2. In a large saucepan over high heat, mix together the heavy cream, 35 grams of sugar, salt, and vanilla and bring to a boil. Once boiling, remove the pan from the heat.

3. In the bowl of a stand mixer fitted with the whisk attachment, whisk the egg yolks and the remaining 35 grams of sugar until pale and thick, 3 to 5 minutes.

4. Temper the egg mixture by mixing in about one-third of the hot cream mixture, whisking constantly until combined. Once the egg mixture is tempered, add it to the remaining hot cream mixture and stir to combine.

5. Place 4 (5-inch) crème brûlée molds or ramekins in a large baking pan. Strain the cream mixture equally into the molds.

6. Place the baking pan with the molds in the oven and fill the baking pan with enough water to reach halfway up the sides of the molds. Cover the pan with aluminum foil and bake for 35 to 40 minutes, or until the crèmes brûlées appear set and jiggle slightly in the center.

7. Transfer the molds to a sheet pan and let cool to room temperature. Place the pan in the refrigerator for at least 4 hours. The custard will firm up even more.

8. Sprinkle a generous amount of sugar over the top of each custard and, using a kitchen torch, broil the sugar until it is melted and turns a deep golden brown. Serve immediately.

Technique Tip: Always temper any egg mixture before adding it to a hot liquid to prevent it from turning into scrambled eggs instead of a smooth, creamy custard.

Doughnuts, Three Ways

Prep time: 1 hour • **Cook time:** 30 to 45 minutes

If you love doughnuts, you understand the big debate between cake doughnuts and yeast doughnuts. While both of them have their merits, I have to say I'm totally on Team Yeast. They have always been my favorite because they are so light and fluffy. The base of these doughnuts is Brioche (page 28) dough. All you need to do is roll out the dough, cut the doughnuts, fry them, and fill or top them with your favorite flavors. • *Yield: 18 to 20 doughnuts*

For the doughnuts

1 recipe Brioche (page 28)
   dough, prepared
   through Day 1
Vegetable or canola oil,
   for frying

For chocolate custard–filled doughnuts

1 recipe Pastry Cream
   (page 46), made with the
   addition of 150 grams
   melted milk chocolate

For vanilla-sugar doughnuts

Vanilla sugar (see
   Technique Tip)

For glazed doughnuts

250 grams
   confectioners' sugar
60 milliliters milk or water
½ teaspoon flavored
   extract (optional)

To make the doughnuts

1. Line a sheet pan with parchment paper. Line a wire rack with paper towels.

2. Roll out the brioche dough to about ½ inch thick.

3. Using a 3-inch round cookie cutter, cut out the dough. (If you would like to make traditional ring doughnuts, use a 1½-inch cookie cutter to cut out the centers.)

4. Place the cut-out dough on the prepared sheet pan and proof until the dough doubles in size, about 1 hour.

5. In a large, deep pot over medium-high heat, add enough oil so that the doughnuts will float when they are frying. Place a candy thermometer in the pot. When the temperature reaches 350°F, the oil is ready for frying.

6. Using a slotted spoon, carefully lower the doughnuts into the hot oil, frying 2 or 3 at a time. Do not over-crowd them. Fry until golden brown, 2 to 3 minutes. Flip the doughnuts over with a fork or wood chopsticks and fry until the other side is golden brown, another 2 to 3 minutes.

7. Using the slotted spoon, transfer the doughnuts to the paper towel–lined wire rack.

To make chocolate custard–filled doughnuts

Let the doughnuts cool completely. Use an Ateco #821 star tip to make a hole in the side of each doughnut. Fill a pastry bag fitted with an Ateco #803 tip with the chocolate pastry cream and fill the doughnuts.

To make vanilla-sugar doughnuts

Place the vanilla sugar in a wide, shallow bowl. While the doughnuts are still warm, roll them in the vanilla sugar.

To make glazed doughnuts

In a small bowl, whisk together the confectioners' sugar, milk, and extract (if using). Dip one flat side of a doughnut into the glaze. Shake it a little to remove any excess and place on the sheet pan. Repeat with the rest of the doughnuts. Let sit for about 5 minutes, or until the glaze has set.

Technique Tips:

- *Making vanilla sugar.* Place a split vanilla bean into a glass jar and fill with granulated sugar. Cover and let sit for a few days before using. The vanilla aroma and flavor will infuse into the sugar.
- *Using a thermometer.* Using a candy thermometer will help you keep the oil at a consistent temperature. If the oil isn't hot enough, the doughnuts will absorb too much oil and will be soggy and greasy.

Mendiants

Prep time: 15 minutes

A chocolate lover's dream, mendiants are coin-size confections studded with fruit and nuts. The flavors change depending on how you top them. Try raisins and cashews or dried apricots and crystallized ginger. It's entirely up to you. They make a lovely gift packed into a candy box tied with a colorful ribbon. • *Yield: About 30 (1-inch) mendiants*

125 grams dark chocolate

125 grams white chocolate

150 grams toppings of
your choice

Optional toppings

Raisins

Chopped dried cranberries

Chopped dried cherries

Chopped dried apricots

Chopped candied orange peel

Chopped crystallized ginger

Cashews

Pistachios

Almonds

Freeze-dried strawberries
or raspberries

Fleur de sel

Shredded coconut

1. Line a sheet pan with parchment paper.

2. Temper the dark and white chocolate separately (see Tempering Chocolate, page 156).

3. Pour the dark and white chocolate into separate pastry bags.

   PRO TIP: When adding looser liquids into a pastry bag, place the bag in a tall glass and fold the edges over the edge of the glass. This will free up both your hands to pour the mixture without making a mess.

4. Cut a small opening at the tip of the pastry bag with the dark chocolate and pipe dime-size rounds on the prepared sheet pan. Repeat with the white chocolate, piping a dime-size amount of the white chocolate on top of the dark chocolate. Use a toothpick to swirl the two chocolates together for a beautiful marble effect. You can also make these bigger, if you'd like.

5. Before the chocolate completely sets, add your desired toppings. Let the chocolates completely set before handling.

6. Store the mendiants in an airtight container in a cool place for up to 6 months.

Truffles

Prep time: 2 hours

Truffles are pretty easy to make, but they pack a punch in terms of elegance and style. They can be elevated with an infusion of raspberry or peppermint, and they can be rolled in a variety of toppings. This is another nice recipe to make and give away as a gift. Everyone will love them. • *Yield: About 35 truffles*

150 grams
   semisweet chocolate
125 milliliters heavy cream
5 grams unsalted butter
½ teaspoon vanilla, raspberry,
   coconut, peppermint, or
   orange extract (optional)
   or 15 grams flavored
   liquor (optional)

Optional toppings

Cocoa powder
Coconut flakes
Sprinkles
Crushed nuts
Crushed cookies
Melted tempered chocolate

1. Place the chocolate in a medium bowl.

2. In a medium saucepan over medium-high heat, bring the heavy cream to a gentle boil. Pour the hot cream over the chocolate and let the chocolate melt for a few minutes without stirring it. Add the butter and extract (if using). Stir until completely combined and the chocolate is fully melted.

3. Set the mixture aside until it sets and firms up, about 20 minutes. If it's taking a while to set, cover the bowl with plastic wrap and refrigerate for 30 minutes.

4. Line a sheet pan with parchment paper.

5. Using a mini ice cream scoop, portion out the truffles and place them on the prepared sheet pan. If you don't have an ice cream scoop, fill a pastry bag fitted with a round tip with the chocolate mixture and pipe them out instead. Refrigerate for about 10 minutes.

6. To decorate the truffles, place your desired toppings into individual bowls. Remove the truffles from the refrigerator and roll them between your palms to create a perfect ball. Then roll each truffle in the bowls to cover with the desired toppings.

7. Store the truffles in an airtight container at room temperature for up to 4 days, in the refrigerator for up to 2 weeks, or in the freezer for up to 1 month. Be sure to thaw the truffles in the refrigerator and not at room temperature or they will develop condensation.

Troubleshooting Tip: If the truffles are melting too much because your hands are too warm, run your hands under cold water and dry them completely before continuing to decorate.

Almond Croissants

Prep time: 15 hours • **Cook time:** 15 to 20 minutes

If your croissants have gone stale, or if you simply want to try this version, this is a great way to save them and add even more delicious flavor. The amounts in this recipe assume that you have 6 croissants left over, but feel free to adjust the amount of almond cream if you would like to make a bigger batch. • *Yield: 6 croissants*

100 grams granulated sugar

113 milliliters water

¼ teaspoon almond extract

6 (1- or 2-day-old) Croissants (page 60)

½ recipe Almond Cream (page 82)

Sliced almonds, for topping

Confectioners' sugar, for topping

1. In a small saucepan over medium heat, combine the sugar and water until the sugar has completely dissolved. Stir in the almond extract and remove from the heat.

2. Cut the croissants in half horizontally and, using a pastry brush, soak the inside of each half of the croissant with the syrup.

3. Preheat the oven to 350°F.

4. Spread a generous layer of almond cream on the bottom half of the croissant. Top with the other half and apply a small amount of almond cream on top in an even layer. Place the croissants on a parchment-lined sheet pan.

5. Sprinkle the top with sliced almonds. Repeat with the rest of the croissants.

6. Bake for 15 to 20 minutes. Let cool and serve with a dusting of confectioners' sugar.

Gougères

Prep time: 10 minutes • **Cook time:** 25 to 30 minutes

After bread, I'd have to say cheese is my next favorite food, making gougères the perfect morsel for me. They're salty, cheesy, and light enough for me to not feel bad about eating too many of them by myself. These are a hit for any party or for just snacking on any time. Add even more Gruyère if you're a cheese lover like me. • *Yield: About 30 small or 20 large gougères*

1 recipe pâte à choux
 (see page 50)
130 grams Gruyère cheese,
 finely grated, divided
Pinch freshly ground
 black pepper
Pinch salt
Pinch nutmeg
1 large egg, beaten, for
 egg wash

1. Line a sheet pan with parchment paper. While the pâte à choux is still warm, mix in 100 grams of cheese, the pepper, salt, and nutmeg.

2. Preheat the oven to 500°F.

3. Spoon the dough into a pastry bag fitted with a round tip (Ateco #805 for small gougères or Ateco #807 for large gougères), and pipe rounds (about ½ inch for small or 1 inch for large) on the prepared sheet pan.

4. Brush each gougère with the egg wash. Sprinkle the remaining 30 grams of cheese over the tops.

5. Place the sheet pan in the oven, turn the oven off, and bake for 15 minutes. Turn the oven back on and set the oven to 350°F. Bake for 10 to 15 minutes, until golden brown.

Substitution Tip: These taste great with many kinds of cheese. Try Parmesan or Emmentaler.

Chapter Four

Pies, Tarts, and Galettes

Summer Peach Galette, page 98 (left)

Tips of the Trade

It's fair to say the shell or crust is what truly makes a great tart or galette. Fillings can be pretty wonderful, but you need a perfect foundation to stand up to whatever it holds inside. These tips will help you get that perfect crust every time.

Overworking the Dough

With pastry doughs, it's important to avoid overworking your dough or the crust will be tough and missing the flaky layers that are the hallmark of a good pie. A good dough will still have bits of butter or fat when you roll it out.

Blind Baking

Whenever you have a filling that does not require cooking or just requires very little cooking, the crust should be prebaked or partially prebaked.

Docking the Shell

Pricking the dough with a fork or a knife before baking will prevent the dough from shrinking or puffing up too much by allowing the release of steam. This is important not only for pies and tarts but also for puff pastry.

Chilling Ingredients

It's so important to make sure that ingredients such as butter, water, and milk are cold when mixing them into the dough. This will keep the fats from melting and preserve those gorgeous layers during baking.

Resting and Cooling Times

Pie and tart shells should always be rested in the refrigerator before being baked. This will allow the fat in your dough to firm up again and not melt too quickly when it's in the oven. Once a shell is baked, always let it cool completely (unless instructed otherwise) before adding any fillings, especially when using any kind of custard.

Mixed Berry Hand Pies, page 86

Pâte Brisée

Prep time: 1 hour

This is my all-time favorite dough for any sort of tart, pie, or galette. Also called a shortcrust pastry dough, it's fast and easy to make, and it works well for either sweet or savory fillings, which is why it's so versatile. Once you master this recipe, you'll be finding any excuse to make this tender and perfectly flaky crust. • *Yield: 2 (8- or 9-inch) pie or tart shells*

250 grams cake flour

½ teaspoon salt

½ teaspoon sugar (or 1 teaspoon, if making a sweet recipe)

125 grams cold unsalted butter, cubed

64 milliliters cold water

1. In the bowl of a stand mixer fitted with the paddle attachment, combine the cake flour, salt, and sugar.

2. Cut in the cold butter by mixing on low speed until the butter is the size of small peas. (Make sure that the butter doesn't melt or become too small in size.)

3. With the mixer on, slowly pour the very cold water into the mixture until the dough is soft and shaggy. You may not use all of the water called for in this recipe.

4. Take a small amount of dough (about the size of a walnut) and place it on a clean work surface. Use the heel of your palm to spread the dough out. This will allow the mixture to fully come together. Repeat this process until you've gone through all the dough. The ingredients should be well homogenized, and the dough should be soft and smooth. Gather the dough together into a disk and wrap in plastic wrap. Refrigerate for at least 30 minutes to let the gluten rest. At this point, the dough is ready to use.

5. The dough can be stored wrapped tightly in plastic wrap in the refrigerator for up to 1 week or frozen for up to 2 months.

Technique Tip: Cake flour has the lowest protein content compared to other flours and will produce the least amount of gluten, leaving you with a tender and flaky crust.

Pâte Sucrée

Prep time: 1 hour

This is a dough made with confectioners' sugar that is used for tarts with sweet fillings. It's so delicious that I've also used it to make cookies. It's a simple process, and the dough comes together quickly. Make it ahead to keep in your refrigerator or freezer and you'll be ready to make pies and tarts on the spur of the moment. • *Yield: 2 (9-inch) pie or tart shells*

166 grams unsalted butter, at room temperature

82 grams confectioners' sugar

2 large eggs, at room temperature

330 grams cake flour

1. In the bowl of a stand mixer fitted with the paddle attachment, combine the butter and confectioners' sugar and mix on medium speed until light, fluffy, and pale in color.

2. Add the eggs, one at a time, and mix on medium speed, letting each one become fully incorporated before adding the next.

3. Add the flour and mix until the ingredients are just combined. The dough should be soft and smooth.

4. Wrap the dough and chill in the refrigerator for at least 30 minutes to 1 hour. Your dough is now ready to use.

Technique Tip: When mixing the dough, make sure to mix just until the ingredients are combined. If you overmix the dough, the crust will be tough after it's baked.

Almond Cream

Prep time: 10 minutes

Almond cream has an array of uses. It's wonderful as the base of a fruit tart, baked into a cake, or used as a filling for croissants. It's a main ingredient in Tarte Bourdaloue (page 94). I also like to make a pocket in the center of a slice of Brioche (page 28), stuff it with almond cream, and make French toast, which can be part of a decadent brunch. The possibilities are endless with this delicious, creamy filling. • *Yield: Enough to fill 1 (8- or 9-inch) tart or pie*

125 grams unsalted butter, at room temperature

125 grams granulated sugar

125 grams almond flour

20 grams cornstarch

2 large eggs

1 teaspoon vanilla extract

15 milliliters dark rum (optional)

1. In the bowl of a stand mixer, combine the butter, sugar, and almond flour and mix on medium speed until light and fluffy.

2. Add the cornstarch and mix until well combined. Add the eggs one at a time, letting each one become fully incorporated before adding the next. Add the vanilla extract and rum (if using), and mix until well combined.

3. Cover the bowl with plastic wrap and refrigerate for up to 1 week. When ready to use, place the almond cream in a stand mixer fitted with the paddle attachment and mix until light and fluffy. At that point, it is ready to use in your recipe of choice.

Substitution Tip: Try using other varieties of nut flour, such as hazelnut flour or cashew flour, for a different flavor.

Mixed Berry Fruit Compote

Prep time: 5 minutes · **Cook time:** 10 to 12 minutes

The best thing about a berry filling—or any other kind of fruit filling for a tart—is that you can essentially make it up as you go. Choose your favorite fruit and be sure to add cinnamon, lemon zest, or another complementary seasoning, along with some sort of thickener, such as cornstarch, to make sure the filling holds together. Depending on the ripeness of your fruit, be sure to adjust the level of sweetness to your liking. · *Yield: Enough to fill 1 (9-inch) tart*

460 grams blueberries

230 grams
   strawberries, chopped

230 grams blackberries
   or raspberries

175 grams granulated sugar

½ teaspoon ground cinnamon

Pinch salt

50 grams cornstarch

60 milliliters water

Zest of 1 lemon

1. In a medium saucepan over low heat, mix together the blueberries, strawberries, blackberries, sugar, cinnamon, and salt and cook until the fruit starts to break down and release their juices, about 5 minutes.

2. In a small bowl, mix together the cornstarch and water to make a slurry and add to the fruit mixture. Add the lemon zest and continue to cook, stirring, until the compote reaches the desired thickness, 5 to 7 minutes.

Technique Tip: If you plan on using the compote in a pie that will be baked in the oven, reserve some of the fruit before making the compote. Add the reserved fruit to the compote mixture right before filling the pie or tart. This will ensure a pleasing range of textures in the finished pie.

Chocolate Bourbon Pecan Pie

Prep time: 10 minutes · **Cook time:** 45 to 50 minutes

Pecan pie is a beloved Southern staple, and this version turns up the volume with chocolate and a kick of bourbon. It's decadent, rich, perfect for any holiday gathering, and easily the best part of any meal. · *Yield: 1 (9-inch) pie*

1 tablespoon butter

285 grams pecans, toasted
and roughly chopped

Pinch salt, plus ½ teaspoon

Flour, for dusting

½ recipe Pâte Brisée (page 80)

2 large eggs, at
room temperature

234 grams corn syrup

28 grams butter, melted

2 tablespoons bourbon

1 tablespoon vanilla extract

115 grams semisweet
chocolate, chopped

1. To toast the pecans, in a small skillet over medium-low heat, melt the butter. Add the pecans and a pinch of salt and cook, stirring frequently, until they become aromatic. Watch carefully because they can burn quickly. Transfer to a plate and let cool.

2. Preheat the oven to 350°F.

3. On a lightly floured work surface, roll out the pâte brisée into a 10-inch circle. Transfer the dough to a 9-inch pie pan, then trim and press the edges with your fingers to create a fluted edge. Place the pan in the refrigerator until ready to use.

4. In a bowl, whisk together the eggs, corn syrup, butter, bourbon, vanilla, and ½ teaspoon of salt. Add the toasted pecans and chocolate and stir to combine.

5. Pour the mixture into the crust and smooth it out into an even layer.

6. Bake for 25 minutes. Place some aluminum foil over the crust to prevent it from burning, then bake for an additional 20 to 25 minutes, or until the filling is just a little jiggly in the center.

7. Let cool on a wire rack for about 20 minutes. Place the pie in the refrigerator and chill for at least 1 hour before serving.

Serving Tip: I like to serve this pie with a dollop of bourbon-flavored whipped cream. Whisk together 227 milliliters heavy whipping cream and 1 tablespoon bourbon until it starts to thicken, then slowly sprinkle in 2 tablespoons granulated sugar. Whisk until it reaches stiff peaks.

Tarte Tatin

Prep time: 20 minutes • **Cook time:** 30 to 35 minutes

This classic one-pan dessert is made by arranging fruit in an oven-safe pan and topping it with puff pastry or pâte brisée. After it's baked, you flip it over onto a serving platter for a truly spectacular presentation. It's traditionally made with apples, but you can make it with any kind of firmer fruit, such as peaches, pears, or plums. • *Yield: 1 (9-inch) tart*

100 grams unsalted butter

6 apples (Granny Smith, Honeycrisp, or Golden Delicious), peeled, cored, and halved

325 grams granulated sugar

Juice of ½ lemon

75 milliliters rum or liquor of choice

Flour, for dusting

140 grams Puff Pastry (page 48) or ½ recipe Pâte Brisée (page 80)

1. Melt the butter in a 9-inch round oven-safe pan over medium heat. Cast-iron skillets work great. Arrange the apples in a single layer, rounded-side down, and cook until the apples have started to brown, 8 to 10 minutes.

2. Sprinkle in the sugar and lemon juice and cook until the sugar starts to caramelize, 5 to 7 minutes. Add the rum. Remove the pan from the heat and cover with aluminum foil. Set aside to cool.

3. Preheat the oven to 350°F.

4. On a lightly floured work surface, roll out the puff pastry into a 10-inch circle. Cut a 9-inch circle out of the dough and dock it with the tines of a fork.

5. Place the dough over the apples in the pan, tucking in the edges as needed.

6. Bake for 30 to 35 minutes, or until the dough is evenly browned and cooked through.

7. Immediately place a serving platter over the pan and flip it over. Serve immediately.

Serving Tip: Serve with a dollop of fresh whipped cream or a scoop of vanilla ice cream.

Mixed Berry Hand Pies

Prep time: 1 hour • **Cook time:** 30 to 35 minutes

What makes a pie even better than a sweet and juicy fruit filling? When it's a cute little pie you can hold in your hand, of course! These are super fun to make and, like many recipes in this book, they're fully customizable with your choice of filling. • *Yield: 6 to 8 hand pies*

1 tablespoon cornstarch

1 tablespoon water

500 grams fresh or frozen
    mixed berries

100 grams granulated sugar

1 tablespoon freshly squeezed
    lemon juice

½ teaspoon vanilla extract

¼ teaspoon salt

¼ teaspoon ground cinnamon

Flour, for dusting

1 recipe Pâte Brisée
    (page 80) or ½ recipe
    Puff Pastry (page 48)

1 large egg, beaten, for
    egg wash

Demerara sugar, for topping

Optional fillings

Pumpkin pie filling

Cinnamon apples

Cherries

Blueberries

Sliced peaches

1. Line a sheet pan with parchment paper.

2. In a small bowl, mix together the cornstarch and water until smooth. Set aside.

3. In a medium saucepan over medium heat, mix together the berries, granulated sugar, lemon juice, vanilla, salt, and cinnamon and cook until the berries begin to break down a bit and release their juices, 4 to 6 minutes. Add the cornstarch mixture and cook, stirring often, until the mixture comes to a boil. Remove from the heat and let the mixture cool completely. It will continue to thicken as it cools. Set aside.

4. Lightly flour a work surface and roll out the dough to about ⅛ inch thick. Using a round cookie cutter or the shape of your choice, cut out as many shapes as you can, making sure there are two pieces for each hand pie. You should have between 12 and 16 pieces.

5. Place half of the cut-out pieces of dough on the prepared sheet pan. Spoon 2 to 3 tablespoons of the mixed berry filling onto the center of each piece of dough. Place another piece of dough on top and, using a fork, crimp the edges closed.

6. With a sharp knife, cut 3 slits on the top of each pie. Brush the egg wash on each of the pies and sprinkle with demerara sugar.

7. Place the pies in the refrigerator to rest for up to 30 minutes. Preheat the oven to 375°F.

8. Bake for 30 to 35 minutes, or until golden brown. Let the pies cool on the pans until they're cool enough to handle.

9. Store the pies in an airtight container in the refrigerator for up to 3 days. To reheat, place them in a 350°F oven for 5 minutes. They also taste great cold or at room temperature.

Technique Tip: If some of the hand pies are browning faster than others, rotate the pans in the oven.

Upgrade Tip: Try one of the optional fillings instead of or in addition to the mixed berries. Or turn these hand pies into a delicious, hearty main dish by using chicken pot pie filling or beef stew for the filling.

Lemon Meringue Tart with Lemon Curd

Prep time: 25 minutes, plus time for curd to cool • **Cook time:** 7 to 10 minutes

When it comes to lemon, the more tart, the better, in my opinion. A lemon meringue tart has the perfect combination of tart and sweet that makes it a favorite summer treat. It's even great in the winter when you're craving something fresh. • *Yield: 1 (9-inch) tart*

For the lemon curd

180 grams unsalted butter

150 grams granulated sugar

145 milliliters freshly squeezed lemon juice

Zest of 3 lemons

3 large eggs

2 large egg yolks

For the crust

½ recipe Pâte Brisée (page 80) or Pâte Sucrée (page 81)

Flour, for dusting

For the Swiss meringue

100 grams granulated sugar

75 grams large egg whites

Pinch salt

To make the lemon curd

1. Line a sheet pan with plastic wrap and set aside.

2. Pour an inch or two of water in a medium saucepan and bring to a simmer over medium heat.

3. In a medium bowl, whisk together the butter, sugar, lemon juice, lemon zest, eggs, and egg yolks until combined. Place the bowl over the pot of simmering water and cook the mixture, whisking constantly until it's thick and coats the back of a spoon.

4. Strain the curd through a fine-mesh strainer directly over the prepared sheet pan and spread it out. Wrap the pan with plastic wrap, making sure the plastic touches the surface of the curd to prevent it from developing a skin. Place in the refrigerator and let cool completely. Whisk the curd before using.

5. The curd can be stored in an airtight container in the refrigerator for up to 3 days.

To make the crust

1. If working with frozen dough, it should be placed in the refrigerator the night before to thaw. Let refrigerated or thawed dough sit on the counter for about 10 minutes before you begin to roll it out. It will require some elbow grease, but it will quickly begin to soften and become easy to roll out.

2. On a lightly floured work surface, roll the dough out into a 10-inch circle about ⅛ inch thick.

3. Line the tart pan with the rolled-out dough and, using a paring knife, cut the excess off the edges. Preheat the oven to 350°F.

4. Place the pan in the refrigerator to chill for 10 minutes.

5. Dock the tart shell with the tines of a fork and blind bake for 7 to 10 minutes, or until the crust is lightly golden brown. Let the shell cool completely on a wire rack.

To make the Swiss meringue and assemble the tart

1. Pour an inch or two of water in a medium saucepan and bring to a simmer over medium heat.

2. In the bowl of a stand mixer fitted with the whisk attachment, combine the sugar and egg whites.

3. Place the bowl over the saucepan of simmering water and heat, whisking frequently, until the mixture is 160°F.

4. Transfer back to the stand mixer and whisk on low speed for about 1 minute. Add the salt, increase the speed to high, and whisk until it reaches stiff peaks.

5. Transfer the meringue to a pastry bag fitted with a pastry tip. I like to use Ateco #805, #824, or #825.

6. Fill the crust with the lemon curd, smoothing it out in an even layer. Pipe the meringue over the lemon curd.

7. Using a kitchen torch, brown the meringue.

8. The lemon meringue tart does not store well and should be eaten the same day it's made.

Technique Tips:

- *Making curd.* Once you feel confident with making lemon curd, you can skip the double boiler and cook directly on the heat, but be careful that it doesn't burn.
- *Making Swiss meringue.* This type of meringue is made by heating the egg whites and sugar over a double boiler before whisking them into stiff peaks. When mixing the Swiss meringue, make sure there is no trace of egg yolk in the egg whites or the meringue will not whip into the stiff peaks that are needed.

Banana Cream Tart

Prep time: 30 minutes • Cook time: 20 minutes

If you're craving something not so incredibly sweet, this is the perfect tart for you. Bonus: It's gluten-free! The crust tastes almost like an oatmeal cookie, and the luscious, creamy filling is something you won't soon forget. • *Yield: 1 (9-inch) tart*

For the crust

Nonstick cooking spray, for greasing the pan
96 grams almond flour
90 grams rolled oats
55 grams unsalted butter, melted
50 grams brown sugar
30 grams almonds, finely chopped
½ teaspoon cinnamon
1 teaspoon vanilla extract
Pinch salt

For the filling

330 grams Pastry Cream (page 46)
15 milliliters rum
½ teaspoon banana extract
350 milliliters heavy cream
35 grams confectioners' sugar
1½ bananas, cut into small pieces

To make the crust

1. Preheat the oven to 350°F. Grease a tart pan with cooking spray.

2. In a medium bowl, mix together the almond flour, oats, butter, brown sugar, almonds, cinnamon, vanilla, and salt.

3. Press the mixture into the tart pan, spreading it evenly across the bottom and sides of the pan.

4. Bake for 20 minutes, or until lightly golden brown. Let cool completely on a wire rack.

To make the filling and assemble the tart

1. In a medium bowl, whisk the pastry cream with the rum and banana extract and set aside.

2. In the bowl of a stand mixer fitted with the whisk attachment, whisk the heavy cream and confectioners' sugar on medium speed until they form stiff peaks. Fold about three-quarters of the whipped cream into the pastry cream. Fold in the bananas.

3. Spread the filling into the cooled tart shell and smooth out evenly. Transfer the remaining whipped cream into a piping bag and pipe into whatever pattern you like.

Technique Tip: It's important to whip the cream to stiff peaks or the filling will be too soft.

Raspberry Chocolate Ganache Tart

Prep time: 45 minutes, plus time for tart shell to cool ◦ **Cook time:** 10 to 12 minutes

The first time I made this tart, I was a teenager. My family went nuts over it, and it's been one of my favorite things to make ever since. The sweetness of the chocolate perfectly complements the tang of the raspberries. ◦ *Yield: 1 (9-inch) tart*

½ recipe Pâte Sucrée (page 81)

Flour, for dusting

170 grams semisweet chocolate, chopped in small pieces

68 grams unsalted butter

22 grams corn syrup

188 milliliters heavy cream

1 teaspoon raspberry extract

1 pint fresh raspberries

1. Preheat the oven to 350°F.

2. Roll out the dough on a lightly floured work surface to a 10-inch circle, about ⅛ inch thick. Line a 9-inch tart pan with the dough, using a paring knife to trim off the excess. Place the pan in the refrigerator for at least 10 minutes.

3. Blind bake the tart shell for 10 to 12 minutes, or until lightly browned. Let cool completely on a wire rack.

4. In a medium bowl, combine the chocolate, butter, and corn syrup and set aside.

5. In a medium saucepan over medium-high heat, bring the heavy cream to a boil. Pour it over the chocolate and let the mixture sit for 1 to 2 minutes. Stir the mixture gently, add the raspberry extract, and mix until well combined.

6. Pour the chocolate ganache into the cooled tart shell and smooth the filling out evenly. Let the tart sit at room temperature until it sets, 20 to 30 minutes. Arrange the fresh raspberries in a concentric circle pattern over the top, or in any design you like.

7. The tart is best eaten the same day it's made, but you can store leftovers covered in plastic wrap in the refrigerator for up to 2 days.

Upgrade Tip: For a little something extra, spread some raspberry jam in the baked tart shell in step 6, just before you pour in the ganache.

Serving Tip: For a fancier look and extra boost of raspberry flavor, in step 6, place the raspberries with the openings face up, and pipe a dot of raspberry jam into each individual raspberry.

Chocolate Bavarian Cream Strawberry Tart

Prep time: 35 minutes • Cook time: 8 to 10 minutes

A tart like this is something you'd make for a special occasion, but let's be real—it's too good to restrict yourself to making it only a few times a year. It's both decadent and refreshing, with its mix of smooth chocolate and sweet strawberries. What I really love about this tart is that you can change up the flavors by switching the chocolate to white, milk, or even dark. And as you probably guessed, you can use different varieties of fruit, as well. In the end, my favorite combination is semisweet chocolate with strawberries. Once you make this tart, I think it will be your favorite, too. • *Yield: 1 (9-inch) tart*

For the Bavarian cream filling

2 sheets gelatin

125 milliliters whole milk

50 grams granulated sugar, divided

2 large egg yolks

50 grams semisweet chocolate, chopped

125 milliliters heavy cream

For the tart

½ recipe Pâte Sucrée (page 81)

Flour, for dusting

200 grams Mixed Berry Fruit Compote (page 83), made with all strawberries

Chocolate curls, for garnish

Sliced strawberries, for garnish

To make the Bavarian cream filling

1. In a shallow bowl, soak the gelatin sheets in cold water and set them aside to soften.

2. In a medium saucepan over medium-high heat, mix together the milk and 25 grams of sugar and bring to a boil. Remove from the heat.

3. In a separate bowl, whisk together the egg yolks and the remaining 25 grams of sugar.

4. Pour one-third of the hot milk mixture into the egg yolk mixture, whisking constantly. Add the tempered egg mixture to the saucepan with the hot milk and return to the heat. Cook over medium heat, stirring continuously, until the custard thickens and coats the back of a spoon and a finger dragged through leaves a line.

   PRO TIP: Make sure to constantly stir the bottom and sides during this step, as such a small amount can burn quickly.

5. Remove the custard from the heat, add the chopped chocolate, and stir to combine.

6. Remove the gelatin sheets from the water, squeezing them to remove any excess water. Add the sheets of gelatin to the warm custard and stir to combine.

7. Fill a large bowl halfway with ice and pour in enough water to cover the ice. Set an empty bowl over the ice.

8. Strain the custard through a fine-mesh strainer directly into the bowl over the ice bath. Stir the custard occasionally to ensure even cooling.

9. In the bowl of a stand mixer fitted with the whisk attachment, whisk the heavy cream until it forms stiff peaks.

10. When the custard is cooled and has thickened to the consistency of pudding, fold in the whipped cream. Use it right away or store in an airtight container in the refrigerator for up to 2 days.

To make the tart

1. Preheat the oven to 350°F.

2. Roll out the dough on a lightly floured work surface into a 10-inch circle about ⅛ inch thick. Line a 9-inch tart pan with the dough, using a paring knife to trim off the excess. Place the pan in the refrigerator for at least 10 minutes.

3. Blind bake for 8 to 10 minutes, or until the shell is lightly browned. Set aside to cool completely.

4. Spread an even layer of the strawberry compote on the bottom of the crust.

5. Pour the Bavarian cream filling over the compote and spread evenly. Place the tart in the refrigerator and chill for at least 15 minutes before decorating.

6. Cover with chocolate curls and sliced strawberries.

7. This tart is best eaten on the day it is made.

Substitution Tip: For a chocolate crust, substitute 30 grams of cocoa powder for 30 grams of flour in the Pâte Sucrée (page 81) and make as instructed.

Tarte Bourdaloue

Prep time: 35 minutes • **Cook time:** 45 to 50 minutes

The first time I ever tried—or even heard of—this classic French tart made with poached pears and almond cream was in my first month of culinary school. Since then, I've been hooked. Not only is it visually beautiful, but it's something a bit unexpected. This makes the perfect fall or winter dessert. • *Yield: 1 (9-inch) tart*

For the poached pears

3 liters white wine

1 kilogram granulated sugar

Juice of 5 lemons

3 vanilla beans, split and scraped, or 3 teaspoons vanilla extract

3 star anise pods

2 cinnamon sticks

3 Bosc or Anjou pears, peeled, halved lengthwise, and cored

For the tart

½ recipe Pâte Brisée (page 80)

Flour, for dusting

1 recipe Almond Cream (page 82)

Raw sliced almonds

¼ cup honey

To make the poached pears

1. In a large saucepan over medium-high heat, combine the wine, sugar, lemon juice, vanilla, star anise, and cinnamon sticks and bring to a boil.

2. Add the pears, lower the heat to medium-low, and simmer, stirring occasionally, until you can pierce a pear with a knife with no resistance, 12 to 15 minutes.

3. Transfer the pears to a plate and cool completely. Let the poaching liquid cool, as well.

4. The pears can be stored in the cooled liquid in the refrigerator for up to 1 week.

To make the tart

1. Roll out the dough on a lightly floured work surface into a 10-inch circle about ⅛ inch thick.

2. Line a 9-inch tart pan with the dough, using a paring knife to trim off the excess. Place the pan in the refrigerator for at least 10 minutes.

3. Dock the bottom of the tart shell.

4. Whisk the almond cream until it's soft and fluffy. Pour it in the tart shell and spread it out evenly.

5. Preheat the oven to 350°F.

6. Cut the pears crosswise into ¼-inch-thick slices. Keeping them "intact," arrange the pear halves on top of the almond cream, fanning them out decoratively. (You should see 6 pear shapes arranged with the narrow ends toward the center and wide ends toward the edge of the tart.)

7. Place the almonds in the areas where the almond cream is showing.

8. Bake for 45 to 50 minutes, or until the almond cream is set, the edges of the pears are caramelized, and the crust is browned.

9. In a microwave-safe bowl, microwave the honey for about 30 seconds. Using a pastry brush, glaze the top of the tart with the honey.

Serving Tip: If you don't plan to serve the tart right away, an unbaked tart can be covered with plastic wrap and refrigerated for up to 2 days or frozen for 1 week.

Technique Tip: Always roll out dough to at least 1 inch larger than your pan. This makes sure that you'll be able to fully cover the sides of the pan, resulting in a perfect-fitting dough every time.

Quiche Lorraine

Prep time: 20 minutes • **Cook time:** 23 to 35 minutes

Any time you're looking for a way to spice up breakfast or serve something elegant for brunch, give this quiche a try. It's also perfect on those breakfast-for-dinner nights, a favorite in my home! Quiche Lorraine is typically made with bacon and cheese, but you can pretty much add whatever meats and vegetables you'd like. • *Yield: 4 (4-inch) tartlets*

½ recipe Pâte Brisée (page 80)

Flour, for dusting

6 slices thick-cut bacon, cut into small pieces

3 large eggs

150 milliliters heavy cream

100 milliliters whole milk

¼ teaspoon freshly ground black pepper

Pinch salt

Pinch nutmeg

60 grams Gruyère cheese, grated

20 grams Parmesan cheese, grated

1. Line a sheet pan with parchment paper.

2. Roll out the dough on a lightly floured work surface to about ⅛ inch thick. Cut the dough into 4 (5-inch) circles. Line 4 (4-inch) tartlet pans with the dough, using a paring knife to trim off the excess, and place on the sheet pan. Place the pan in the refrigerator for at least 10 minutes.

3. Preheat the oven to 350°F. Dock the bottoms of the tartlet shells. Be careful not to puncture the dough too much or the egg filling will seep through.

4. Blind bake the tartlet shells for 8 to 10 minutes, or until lightly browned. Set aside on a wire rack to cool.

5. Lower the oven temperature to 250°F.

6. Line a plate with paper towels. In a small skillet over medium heat, cook the bacon until the fat is rendered and the bacon is lightly browned, about 6 to 8 minutes. Transfer the bacon to the paper towel–lined plate and set aside to cool.

7. In a medium bowl, whisk together the eggs, cream, milk, pepper, salt, and nutmeg. Strain the mixture through a fine-mesh strainer and set aside.

8. Scatter the bacon equally among the cooled tart shells. Sprinkle the Gruyère and Parmesan equally among the tart shells, then pour the egg mixture into each shell.

9. Bake for 15 to 25 minutes, or until the custard is set and a knife inserted in the middle comes out clean.

Serving Tip: For breakfast, serve with a side of home fries. For lunch, serve with a side salad.

Technique Tip: Be sure to bake immediately after filling with the egg mixture or the tart shells will start to soften.

Substitution Tip: Try one or more of these ingredients to change up the flavors of your quiche:

- Sliced mushrooms
- Chopped spinach
- Chopped tomatoes
- Chopped bell peppers
- Sliced leeks
- Sliced boiled potatoes
- Chopped onions
- Crumbled cooked sausage
- Chopped ham
- Sliced jalapeño peppers
- Shredded Swiss cheese
- Shredded cheddar cheese

Summary Peach Galette

Prep time: 30 minutes • Cook time: 25 to 30 minutes

This is one of my favorite summer desserts. Galettes are wonderful because you can change the fruit to whatever you'd like and what's in season and you don't need a pie pan or tart pan to make it. It's a really simple and delicious dessert that you can make at a moment's notice, but it's still special enough to wow your guests. • *Yield: 1 (9-inch) galette*

½ recipe Pâte Brisée (page 80)

Flour, for dusting

5 peaches, cut into
  ½-inch-thick slices

40 grams brown sugar

25 grams unsalted butter

1 teaspoon ground cinnamon

½ teaspoon ground ginger

Juice of ½ lemon

Pinch salt

1 large egg, beaten, for
  egg wash

Demerara sugar, for topping

Ice cream, for
  serving (optional)

Whipped cream, for
  serving (optional)

1. Line a sheet pan with parchment paper.

2. Roll out the dough on a lightly floured work surface into a 10-inch circle, about ⅛ inch thick. Transfer the rolled-out dough to the prepared sheet pan and place it in the refrigerator.

3. In a medium sauté pan over low heat, mix together the peaches, brown sugar, butter, cinnamon, ginger, lemon juice, and salt and cook until the peaches are slightly tender. Remove from the heat and let cool completely.

4. Preheat the oven to 350°F.

5. Arrange the cooled peaches on top of the rolled-out dough, and fold the dough toward the center all the way around, leaving most of the filling showing.

6. Brush the edges of the dough with the egg wash and sprinkle with demerara sugar.

7. Bake for 25 to 30 minutes, or until the edges are nicely browned and the peaches are tender.

8. Serve warm with a scoop of ice cream or a dollop of whipped cream (if using).

Technique Tip: When cooking the peaches on the stove, I like to cook them just until they are soft enough to cut with a fork but still have a bit of bite to them. They will continue to cook in the oven, so you're only looking to soften them a bit. If your peaches are very ripe, skip the cooking step and just combine the fruit with the other ingredients in a bowl.

Rustic Tomato Galette

Prep time: 40 minutes, plus time for onions to cool • **Cook time:** 10 to 15 minutes

Sometimes a delicious savory tart can really hit the spot. Like most tarts, you can play around with the ingredients and add whatever veggies or cheeses you already have in the refrigerator. This tart also makes the perfect simple dinner, with plenty of leftovers for lunch the next day. • *Yield: 1 (9-inch) galette*

½ recipe Pâte Brisée (page 80)

Flour, for dusting

28 grams unsalted butter

2 white onions, thinly sliced

1 tablespoon chopped garlic

¼ teaspoon salt, plus more for seasoning

¼ teaspoon dried oregano

¼ teaspoon freshly ground black pepper, plus more for seasoning

3 heirloom tomatoes, sliced

55 grams blue cheese or Parmesan cheese

30 grams pine nuts

4 slices crumbled cooked bacon (optional)

1. Line a sheet pan with parchment paper.

2. Roll the dough on a lightly floured work surface into a 10-inch circle about ⅛ inch thick. Place the rolled-out dough on the prepared sheet pan and refrigerate for at least 10 minutes.

3. In a medium sauté pan over low heat, melt the butter. Add the onions, garlic, salt, oregano, and pepper. Cook, stirring occasionally, until the onions are extremely soft and caramelized, 35 to 40 minutes. Set aside to cool.

4. Arrange the onions on top of the rolled-out dough and fold the dough over toward the center all the way around, leaving most of the filling showing.

5. Preheat the oven to 350°F.

6. Arrange the sliced tomatoes, blue cheese, pine nuts, and bacon (if using) on top of the galette. Season with salt and pepper.

7. Bake for 10 to 15 minutes, or until the crust is nicely browned.

8. This tart is best eaten the same day it's made.

Technique Tip: To caramelize onions, they need to cook very slowly over low heat, which will take a long time, but they will be extremely sweet and delicious. If you try to cook them faster at a higher temperature, they will cook too quickly and become bitter.

Cakes and Cupcakes

Black Forest Cake, page 116 (left)

Tips of the Trade

There are several factors that make a cake delicious. You want it to be moist and full of flavor but not too sweet, and there must be a nice ratio of cake to frosting. I take my cakes very seriously—with these tips, you'll be sure to have a beautiful and, more important, delicious centerpiece for any party.

Cake Assembly

To make this process a lot easier, be sure your cakes are chilled before you decorate them. Place all your cake layers in the refrigerator or even the freezer for at least a couple of hours, or overnight. This helps make the cakes a lot sturdier when slicing layers to fill.

Storage

Once your cake has been fully iced, store it in the refrigerator until you are ready to serve it. Let the cake come to room temperature before serving, especially if it's been covered and filled with buttercream. You need to allow the butter to come back to room temperature before you can cut through the cake with ease.

Never Overmix!

There is a reason a lot of cake recipes use cake flour. It's because cake flour has the lowest gluten content, which generally results in a lighter and fluffier cake. This won't save you if you overmix, though. Overmixing will result in a tough and very dense, almost chewy cake.

Portioning Cupcakes

My favorite tip for making cupcakes is to use an ice cream scoop or a cookie scoop to fill the cupcake pan with equal portions of batter. There's nothing more disappointing than to have a dozen different-sized cupcakes. Using a scoop will ensure that your cupcakes will be the same size and that they will all cook evenly. (This works great for muffins, too!)

Sift Your Ingredients

It's important to sift the dry ingredients when you're making cakes. You don't want to have any lumps in your batter, and you don't want to run the risk of overmixing your batter when you do see them. Take the time for this step and you'll be sure to always have a light, lump-free cake!

Swiss Meringue Buttercream

Prep time: 45 minutes

Every baker or cakemaker has their preference when it comes to buttercream. Swiss meringue happens to be my personal favorite because the buttercream is so light and smooth. It's super easy once you get the hang of it, and you can use it for any kind of cake. • *Yield: Enough to fill and frost 1 (8-inch) round cake*

570 grams granulated sugar

330 grams large egg whites

Pinch salt

900 grams unsalted butter, cubed, at room temperature

1. Pour an inch or two of water into a medium saucepan and bring to a simmer over medium heat.

2. In the bowl of a stand mixer, combine the sugar and egg whites with a hand whisk.

   PRO TIP: Separate the egg whites into a separate bowl and then add them to the bowl with the sugar. It's important that not even the smallest amount of egg yolk is mixed in with the whites or the meringue won't develop. Also, make sure the bowl you are using is completely clean and there is no fat residue present.

3. Place the bowl over the saucepan of simmering water and heat, whisking frequently, until the mixture reaches 130°F to 140°F on a candy thermometer.

4. Transfer the bowl to the stand mixer and whisk with the whisk attachment on low for about 1 minute. Add the salt, increase the speed to high, and whisk until it doubles in volume and reaches stiff peaks.

5. With the mixer on low, add the cubed butter, piece by piece, and continue to whisk. Once all the butter has been added, increase the speed to high and mix until the buttercream is light and fluffy.

6. If you'd like to add more flavor to your buttercream, add those ingredients now (see Variation Tip). Change to the paddle attachment and beat until well combined.

Troubleshooting Tip: If your buttercream is too loose and won't come together, it means it was too warm when you were adding the butter. You can save it, though! Just place it in the refrigerator for 20 minutes to let it solidify a bit, then mix it in a stand mixer until light and fluffy.

Technique Tip: It's best to make buttercream right before you plan to use it. I never make buttercream more than 1 day before serving, but you can make it up to 2 days in advance. You can also freeze leftover buttercream for up to 2 weeks. Place it in the refrigerator overnight to defrost and then beat it in a stand mixer until fluffy before using.

Variation Tip: When flavoring my buttercream, I add these various additions depending on what I'm making. Add a small amount, a little at a time, and taste as you add until you reach the desired intensity of flavor.

- Peanut butter
- Melted chocolate
- Vanilla bean/vanilla paste/vanilla extract
- Raspberry, lemon, peppermint, orange, coconut, or other extract
- Lemon curd
- Dulce de leche
- Fruit purées
- Nutella
- Crushed cookies
- Maple syrup
- Cinnamon

Mirror Glaze

Mirror glazes have become quite popular as a spectacular way to cover cakes. With so many color options and the abstract quality they create, no two cakes are ever the same. Let your imagination run wild and have fun with it. • *Yield: Enough to glaze 2 (8-inch) round cakes*

116 grams white chocolate,
  chopped into pieces
3½ gelatin sheets
100 grams granulated sugar
66 grams condensed milk
50 milliliters water, plus more
  for soaking the gelatin
Gel food coloring of choice

1. Place the white chocolate in a bowl.

2. In a shallow bowl, soak the gelatin sheets in cold water and set aside to soften.

3. In a medium saucepan over medium heat, combine the sugar, condensed milk, and water and cook until the sugar is completely dissolved. Turn off the heat, add the softened gelatin, and stir to combine.

4. Pour the mixture over the chocolate and set aside until the chocolate melts, about 5 minutes. Using an immersion blender, blend until smooth.

5. Place a thermometer in the bowl and let the glaze cool until it's between 90°F and 94°F. At this point, add the food coloring and blend with the immersion blender.

6. The glaze can be stored in an airtight container in the refrigerator for up to 3 days. To use, reheat it on the stovetop until it reaches between 90°F and 94°F.

Technique Tips:

- *Cooling glaze.* To cool the glaze more quickly, place the bowl of glaze over an ice bath and stir constantly until it reaches the desired temperature.

- *Glazing.* Mirror glazes work best when the cake is frozen. Start with a fully frosted cake that is as smooth as possible, and freeze it for 30 minutes. Once the cake is frozen, place a wire rack over a sheet pan. Place the cake on the wire rack and pour the glaze slowly over the top, making sure to cover the entire cake.

Cream Cheese Frosting

Prep time: 15 minutes

Cream cheese frosting is a great choice for icing lots of different cakes, though traditionally it's used for red velvet or carrot cakes. Try it on spiced cakes or chocolate cakes. There really are no rules when it comes to cake! With some slight adjustments, you can easily change the flavor to suit whatever cake you choose to pair it with (see Variation Tip). • *Yield: Enough to fill and frost 1 (8-inch) round cake*

450 grams cream cheese

350 grams
confectioners' sugar

200 grams unsalted butter

30 grams sour cream

1 teaspoon vanilla extract

Zest of 1 lemon

1. In the bowl of a stand mixer fitted with the paddle attachment, combine the cream cheese, confectioners' sugar, and butter and mix until completely smooth.

2. Add the sour cream, vanilla, and lemon zest and mix on medium speed until smooth and fluffy.

Technique Tip: It's important to make sure the confectioners' sugar is fully incorporated into the butter or the frosting will be lumpy.

Variation Tips:

- *Fruit-flavored frosting.* To make a fruit-flavored frosting, add 1 teaspoon of your favorite extract. I prefer orange or raspberry.
- *Chocolate frosting.* To make chocolate frosting, omit the lemon zest and add 65 grams of cocoa powder with the sour cream.
- *Cinnamon frosting*: To make cinnamon frosting, omit the lemon zest and add 1 tablespoon of ground cinnamon with the sour cream.

Orange Pound Cake

Prep time: 10 minutes · Cook time: 50 minutes to 1 hour

Traditionally, pound cake was literally one pound each of sugar, butter, and flour. I've actually tried that recipe before, and let's just say it wasn't the most delicious cake I've ever had. This recipe offers a nicer balance and a refreshing burst of orange flavor. You can easily leave it out or add lemon instead. · *Yield: 1 (9-by-5-inch) cake*

100 grams unsalted butter, melted, plus more for greasing the pan

200 grams cake flour, plus more for dusting

4 grams baking powder

220 grams granulated sugar

120 grams sour cream

Zest of 2 oranges

4 large eggs

1 orange, segmented into supremes

120 grams confectioners' sugar

30 milliliters orange juice

1. Preheat the oven to 325°F. Grease and flour a 9-by-5-inch loaf pan. Set aside.

2. In a bowl, sift together the flour and baking powder. Set aside.

3. In a separate large bowl, combine the sugar, sour cream, orange zest, and eggs.

4. Fold the dry ingredients into the wet ingredients until just combined. Be mindful not to overmix or the cake will not be the correct texture.

5. Add the melted butter and orange supremes and stir to combine. Pour the mixture into the prepared loaf pan and spread out evenly.

6. Bake for 50 minutes to 1 hour, until a toothpick inserted into the middle of the cake comes out clean. Let cool on a wire rack for 5 minutes, then unmold and let cool completely.

7. To make the glaze, in a small bowl, mix together the confectioners' sugar and orange juice until smooth.

8. Place the warm cake on a serving plate and drizzle the glaze over the top.

Angel Food Cake

Prep time: 20 minutes • **Cook time:** 35 to 40 minutes

One of the most basic cakes—and highly underrated in my opinion—angel food cake is the perfect base for so many fillings and toppings. My favorite thing to do with it, though, is to layer it in a trifle with berries and lemon curd. Whether you pair it with fruit, ice cream, or mousse, this cake makes a delicious and surprisingly light dessert. • *Yield: 1 (10-inch) cake*

145 grams cake flour

100 grams confectioners' sugar

400 grams large egg whites

Pinch salt

200 grams granulated sugar

1 teaspoon cream of tartar

¼ teaspoon vanilla extract

¼ teaspoon almond extract (or raspberry, orange, or lemon extract)

1. Preheat the oven to 325°F.

2. In a medium bowl, whisk together the flour and confectioners' sugar and set aside.

3. In the bowl of a stand mixer fitted with the whisk attachment, combine the egg whites and salt and whisk until foamy. With the mixer running, slowly add the granulated sugar and cream of tartar and whisk until the mixture reaches stiff peaks.

4. Add the vanilla and almond extracts and fold in once; it's okay to leave it streaky.

5. Fold the flour mixture into the meringue a little at a time, folding just enough to combine the ingredients.

6. Pour the batter into an ungreased angel food cake pan and run a knife through the batter to release any air pockets.

7. Bake for 35 to 40 minutes, or until lightly browned and firm to the touch.

8. Let the cake cool completely in the pan before unmolding.

Serving Tip: Dust the cake lightly with confectioners' sugar or serve alongside Mixed Berry Fruit Compote (page 83) or ice cream.

Technique Tip: It's okay to leave the dry ingredients streaky after each addition to the meringue. If you overmix, the meringue will deflate and the cake will not puff nicely.

Variation Tip: To make a trifle, layer the cake with lemon curd or whipped cream and your favorite macerated berries in a trifle bowl or in mason jars (so cute!) and repeat until the containers are filled.

Vanilla Cake

Prep time: 15 minutes • **Cook time:** 35 to 40 minutes for cake layers,
or 12 to 15 minutes for cupcakes

This is the most requested flavor in my business and with good reason. It may be simple, but it's classic and delicious. It also serves as a perfect base for when you want homemade buttercream to be the star. • *Yield: 2 (8-inch) cake layers or 24 to 26 cupcakes*

226 grams unsalted
butter, plus more for
greasing the pan

368 grams cake flour, plus
more for dusting

3 large eggs, at
room temperature

288 milliliters whole
milk, divided

1½ tablespoons vanilla extract

84 milliliters vegetable oil
(omit for cupcakes)

368 grams granulated sugar

4 teaspoons baking powder

¼ teaspoon baking soda

½ teaspoon salt

1. Preheat the oven to 350°F. Butter and flour 2 (8-inch) cake pans and line the bottoms with parchment paper.

2. In a medium bowl, mix together the eggs, 144 milliliters of milk, and the vanilla and set aside.

3. In another medium bowl, mix together the remaining 144 milliliters of milk and the vegetable oil and set aside.

4. In the bowl of a stand mixer fitted with the paddle attachment, add the flour, sugar, butter, baking powder, baking soda, and salt and mix on low speed until the mixture looks like coarse sand.

5. Add the milk and oil mixture and mix on medium speed for 2 minutes.

6. Add the egg mixture in three parts, mixing completely after each addition. Scrape the sides and bottom of the bowl down and stir to make sure everything is well combined after each addition.

7. Pour the batter equally into 2 (8-inch) cake pans. Bake for 35 to 40 minutes, or until a toothpick inserted into the center of the cake comes out clean. Cool for 5 minutes in the pans before unmolding and cooling completely on a wire rack.

To make cupcakes

Preheat the oven to 325°F. Prepare the batter as directed, but omit the oil. Place cupcake liners in 2 (12-cup) cupcake pans. Fill each liner about three-fourths full with the batter. Bake for 12 to 15 minutes, or until a toothpick inserted into the center of the cake comes out clean.

Technique Tip: Be careful not to overmix the batter or you'll end up with something that looks like dough and your cake will have a dense and gummy texture.

Devil's Food Cake

Prep time: 15 minutes · **Cook time:** 50 minutes for cake layers, or 18 to 20 minutes for cupcakes

This has to be, hands down, my favorite cake ever! It is super moist and super chocolaty but not overly sweet. I promise you'll be able to convert anyone who normally prefers vanilla into a chocolate cake lover. · *Yield: 2 (8-inch) cake layers, 3 (6-inch) cake layers, or 18 to 20 cupcakes*

Butter, for greasing the pans

280 grams all-purpose flour, plus more for dusting

450 grams granulated sugar

100 grams unsweetened cocoa powder

2 teaspoons baking soda

1 teaspoon baking powder

1 teaspoon salt

237 milliliters vegetable oil

237 milliliters whole milk

237 milliliters hot coffee

2 large eggs

1 teaspoon vanilla extract

1. Butter and flour 2 (8-inch) cake pans or 3 (6-inch) cake pans and line the bottoms with parchment paper, or place cupcake liners in 2 (12-cup) cupcake pans.

2. Preheat the oven to 325°F.

3. In the bowl of a stand mixer, sift together the flour, sugar, cocoa powder, baking soda, baking powder, and salt.

4. Add the oil, milk, and coffee and mix at medium speed for 2 minutes.

5. Add the eggs and vanilla and mix at medium speed for another 2 minutes.

6. Pour the batter into the pans and bake for 50 minutes, or until a toothpick inserted into the center of the cake comes out clean.

7. Let the cakes cool in their pans for 10 to 15 minutes, unmold, and let cool completely on wire racks.

Serving Tip: My favorite buttercreams for this cake are raspberry, Nutella, peanut butter, cookies and cream, and classic vanilla.

Troubleshooting Tip: The batter for this cake is supposed to be very thin!

Naked Cake with Ganache Drip

Prep time: 1 hour

Naked cakes—cakes only lightly frosted to show the cake underneath—have become one of the biggest trends in the cake world, and it's easy to see why. They're incredibly simple but also incredibly beautiful. The layers speak for themselves and can be easily dressed up with fresh flowers and a simple ganache drip, another cool trend that's here to stay. • *Yield: 1 (6-inch) 3-layer cake*

200 grams granulated sugar

236 milliliters water

1 recipe Devil's Food Cake (page 111) or Vanilla Cake (page 110), made as 3 (6-inch) layers

½ recipe Swiss Meringue Buttercream (page 104), divided, and flavored however you like

112 grams chocolate, chopped

112 grams heavy cream

40 grams corn syrup

Gel food coloring (optional)

Organic, pesticide-free fresh flowers, for decorating

1. In a small saucepan over medium-high heat, mix together the sugar and water and bring to a boil. Lower the heat to medium-low and cook until the sugar is completely dissolved.

2. Trim the top of each cake layer, removing only enough cake to make the top flat and even. Brush the cake layers with the sugar syrup from the saucepan.

3. Place 1 teaspoon of buttercream on the center of a cake board or cake stand. Place the first layer of cake on top of the buttercream. This will keep the cake from slipping.

4. Spread a layer of buttercream on top of the cake, about ¼ inch thick.

5. Repeat with the remaining cake layers. Place the cake in the refrigerator to let the buttercream set for about 20 minutes.

6. To ice the outside of the cake, apply a small amount of buttercream around the cake and smooth, making sure to let the cake layers show through. Place the cake back in the refrigerator to firm up. It's important for the cake to be cold before you apply the ganache drip.

7. Place the chopped chocolate in a bowl and set aside.

8. In a small saucepan over low heat, mix together the heavy cream and corn syrup and cook, stirring continuously, until small bubbles form around the edges of the pot.

9. Pour the cream mixture over the chocolate and let sit for 2 minutes. Gently stir to combine. If using white chocolate, add gel food coloring (if using).

10. Place the ganache in the refrigerator for about 10 minutes to cool down.

11. Using a spoon, drip some ganache down the sides of the cake.

    PRO TIP: Make sure the cake is cold, which will keep the ganache from dripping right off the cake. Also, if you have one, transfer the ganache to a squeeze bottle for a perfect drizzle over the cake.

12. Pour the rest of the ganache on top of the cake and use a spatula to spread it out evenly. Decorate the cake with fresh flowers.

Technique Tip: If your cake has a fruit filling, candy pieces, or a buttercream that has cookie chunks in it, create a dam around the edge of each cake layer using plain buttercream (you may need to reserve plain buttercream before adding any solid pieces to it). This will keep the fruit or candy inside the cake, and the outside of the finished cake will look smooth and beautiful.

Spice Cake with Apple Compote and Cream Cheese Frosting

Prep time: 15 minutes • **Cook time:** 35 to 40 minutes

This is one of those cakes that I look forward to making every fall and winter (although I have no idea why I wait until then because it deserves to be made year-round). Made with spices like cinnamon, nutmeg, ginger, allspice, and cloves, this cake will fill your entire home with intoxicating aromas. • *Yield: 1 (8-inch) 2-layer cake*

For the apple compote

30 grams unsalted butter

4 apples, peeled, cored, and cubed

Juice of ½ lemon

60 grams brown sugar

1 teaspoon cinnamon

¼ teaspoon allspice

For the cake

226 grams unsalted butter, plus more for greasing the pans

368 grams cake flour, plus more for flouring the pans

3 large eggs, at room temperature

2 large egg yolks, at room temperature

288 milliliters milk, divided

1 tablespoon vanilla extract

84 milliliters vegetable oil

368 grams dark brown sugar

4 teaspoons baking powder

2½ teaspoons ground cinnamon

To make the apple compote

In a large saucepan over medium heat, melt the butter. Add the apples, lemon juice, brown sugar, cinnamon, and allspice and cook until the apples are softened but not completely broken down. Set aside and cool completely.

To make the cake

1. Preheat the oven to 350°F. Butter and flour 2 (8-inch) cake pans and line the bottoms with parchment paper.

2. Place the eggs, egg yolks, 144 milliliters of milk, and vanilla in a bowl and set aside.

3. In another medium bowl, mix together the remaining 144 milliliters of milk and oil and set aside.

4. In the bowl of a stand mixer, combine the flour, brown sugar, butter, baking powder, cinnamon, nutmeg, ginger, allspice, salt, cloves, cardamom, and baking soda and mix on low speed until that the mixture looks like coarse sand.

5. Add the milk and oil mixture and mix on medium speed for 2 minutes.

6. Add the egg mixture in three parts, mixing completely after each addition. Scrape the sides and bottom of the bowl to make sure everything is well combined. Fold in the chopped pecans.

7. Pour the batter equally into 2 (8-inch) cake pans. (There may be a little batter left. You can use it to make 2 or 3 cupcakes if you like.)

8. Bake for 35 to 40 minutes, or until a toothpick inserted into the center of a cake comes out clean. Cool the cakes in the pans for about 4 minutes and then unmold and let cool completely on a wire rack.

1 teaspoon ground nutmeg

1 teaspoon ground ginger

½ teaspoon allspice

½ teaspoon salt

¼ teaspoon ground cloves

¼ teaspoon
   ground cardamom

¼ teaspoon baking soda

125 grams chopped
   pecans, plus more for
   decoration (optional)

200 grams sugar

236 milliliters water

1½ recipes Cream Cheese
   Frosting (page 107)

To assemble the cake

1. In a small saucepan over medium-high heat, mix together the sugar and water and bring to a boil. Lower the heat to medium-low and cook until the sugar is completely dissolved.

2. Using a serrated knife, cut each cake layer horizontally in half, leaving you with 4 layers.

3. Brush the cut side of each cake layer with the simple syrup. Store any remaining simple syrup in an airtight container in the refrigerator for up to 2 weeks.

4. Place 1 cake layer, cut-side up, on a cake round or serving plate.

5. Spread a ½-inch-thick layer of cream cheese frosting over the cake layer. Fill a piping bag fitted with a round tip with some of the cream cheese frosting. Pipe a thick line of frosting around the edge of the cake layer to create a dam. This will prevent the filling from seeping out. Add about 3 tablespoons of the apple compote on top of the cream cheese frosting layer, and spread evenly.

6. Repeat for the second layer.

7. Spread a thin crumb coat (see page 159) of frosting around the outside of the cake and place the cake in the refrigerator for at least 20 minutes.

8. Spread the remaining frosting over the crumb coat until the cake is evenly covered.

9. Pipe additional designs on top of the cake with any leftover frosting or decorate the sides of the cake with chopped pecans (if using).

Technique Tip: Once the cakes have cooled, I like to wrap them in plastic wrap and place them in the refrigerator for at least 2 hours or, even better, overnight. This makes them more stable for layering and frosting.

Variation Tip: For even more spice flavor, make cinnamon frosting, which can be found in the Variation Tip on page 107.

Black Forest Cake

Prep time: 1 hour

I've always loved chocolate and fruit together, so naturally, black forest cake is a favorite of mine. The slightly tart cherries contrast so nicely with the rich chocolate and light creamy layers of whipped cream. I love making this as a special-occasion cake for anyone who loves the classics. • *Yield: 1 (6-inch) 3-layer cake*

For the cherry compote

400 grams fresh or
   frozen cherries
100 grams granulated sugar
1 teaspoon cornstarch
2 teaspoons water
25 milliliters kirsch

For the whipped cream

2 sheets gelatin
450 milliliters heavy cream
100 grams confectioners' sugar

For the cake

200 grams granulated sugar
236 milliliters water
Splash kirsch
1 recipe Devil's Food Cake
   (page 111), made as
   3 (6-inch) layers
Chocolate shavings, for garnish
Fresh cherries, for garnish

To make the cherry compote

1. In a medium saucepan over medium heat, mix together the cherries and sugar and cook until the cherries soften and begin to break down, about 5 minutes. There should still be some whole cherries.

2. In a small bowl, mix together the cornstarch and water until smooth. Add the cornstarch mixture and kirsch to the cherries and cook, stirring, until the mixture thickens.

3. Remove from the heat and let cool.

To make the whipped cream

1. In a shallow bowl, soak the gelatin in cold water.

2. Gently squeeze any excess moisture from the gelatin. Place the softened gelatin in a microwave-safe bowl and microwave until melted, 20 to 30 seconds.

3. In the bowl of a stand mixer fitted with a whisk attachment, combine the heavy cream, confectioners' sugar, and gelatin and whisk until it reaches stiff peaks. Set aside.

To assemble the cake

1. In a small saucepan over medium-high heat, mix together the sugar, water, and kirsch and bring to a boil. Lower the heat to medium-low and cook until the sugar is completely dissolved.

2. Using a serrated knife, cut a very thin layer across the top of each cake layer, just to make them even in height.

3. Brush the cut side of each cake layer with the sugar syrup.

4. Place 1 cake layer, cut-side up, on a cake round or serving plate.

5. Spread a ½-inch-thick layer of whipped cream over the cake layer. Fill a piping bag fitted with a round tip with some of the whipped cream. Pipe a thick line of whipped cream around the edge of the cake layer to create a dam. This will prevent the cherry compote from seeping out.

6. Add about 3 tablespoons of the cherry compote on top of the whipped cream layer and spread evenly.

7. Repeat this process until you've stacked each layer.

8. Spread a thin crumb coat of whipped cream all around the cake and place it in the refrigerator for at least 20 minutes.

9. Remove the cake from the refrigerator and spread whipped cream over the crumb coat until the cake is evenly frosted.

10. Decorate with chocolate shavings and cherries on top of the cake.

Variation Tip: If you don't have 6-inch pans, this recipe can be made into an 8-inch 2-layer cake.

Crêpe Cake

Prep time: 3 hours • **Cook time:** 15 minutes

Are they dessert? Are they breakfast? Who cares? Here is an amazing way to use crêpes to make a stunning cake. • *Yield: 1 (6-inch) 18-layer cake*

For the crêpes

375 milliliters milk

216 grams all-purpose flour

126 grams unsalted butter,
   melted, plus more for
   the skillet

9 large eggs

6 teaspoons granulated sugar

1½ teaspoons vanilla extract

¾ teaspoon salt

Zest of 3 oranges or
   lemons (optional)

For the filling

250 milliliters heavy cream

1 recipe Pastry Cream
   (page 46)

Confectioners' sugar,
   for serving

Berries, for serving

To make the crêpes

1. In a blender or food processor combine the milk, flour, butter, eggs, sugar, vanilla, salt, and orange zest (if using). Blend, scraping down the sides as needed, until smooth.

2. Transfer the mixture to a bowl, cover, and refrigerate for 1 hour.

3. In a 6-inch skillet over medium heat, melt a small amount of butter. Ladle about ¼ cup of batter into the pan and immediately swirl the pan in a circular motion so that the batter covers the bottom.

4. Cook until golden brown on the bottom, 1 to 2 minutes. Using an offset spatula, lift the edges of the crêpe and flip it over. Cook for another 30 seconds.

5. Transfer the crêpe to a wire rack to cool. Repeat the process until there is no batter left. Set the crêpes aside.

To make the filling

1. In the bowl of a stand mixer fitted with the whisk attachment, whisk the heavy cream until it reaches stiff peaks.

2. Whisk the pastry cream to loosen it up. Add about one-third of the whipped cream and fold it into the pastry cream. Fold in the remaining whipped cream, taking care not to deflate the whipped cream.

To assemble the cake

1. Line a 6-inch cake pan with plastic wrap.

2. Place one of the crêpes in the cake pan. Spread a thin layer of the filling over top. Repeat the process with the rest of the crêpes and filling, ending with a crêpe.

3. Place a small plate on top of the cake and place something heavy on top. Place it in the refrigerator and let it set for at least 2 hours.

4. To serve, place a serving platter over the top of the cake pan. Holding the platter and pan together, flip them over. Remove the cake pan and plastic wrap. Dust the top of the cake with confectioners' sugar and berries.

Serving Tip: The crêpes are amazing as individual desserts. Fill individual crêpes with fresh fruit, jam, whipped cream, Nutella, or caramel sauce. Serve warm.

Substitution Tip: To make chocolate crêpes, substitute 45 grams of unsweetened cocoa powder for 45 grams of the flour. Flavor the pastry cream with melted chocolate, lemon extract, coconut extract, or orange extract for additional flavor.

Yule Log

Also known as a *Bûche de Noël*, this is a rolled cake that is often decorated to look like a yule log. For years, whenever I thought of a rolled cake, I automatically thought of those little snack cakes my mom put in my lunch box when I was a kid. Now I think of this classic French holiday cake, and it's one of my favorite things to make every holiday season to share with family and friends. • *Yield: 1 (10-inch) cake*

For the cake

60 grams unsalted butter, melted and cooled to room temperature, plus more for greasing the pan

4 large eggs, separated

Pinch salt

325 grams granulated sugar, divided

125 grams sifted cake flour

236 grams water

For the buttercream

500 grams chocolate, melted

1 recipe Swiss Meringue Buttercream (page 104), divided evenly between 2 bowls

Optional decorations

Confectioners' sugar "snow"

Meringue "mushrooms"

Swiss Meringue Buttercream (page 104), tinted red, for piping into berry shapes

Swiss Meringue Buttercream (page 104), tinted green, for piping into pine stem shapes

To make the cake

1. Preheat the oven to 350°F. Butter a sheet pan and line it with parchment paper, making sure that the parchment overhangs the sides a bit.

2. In the bowl of a stand mixer fitted with the whisk attachment, combine the egg whites, salt, and 125 grams of sugar and whisk until it reaches stiff peaks.

3. Fold the egg yolks and cake flour into the meringue, making sure not to overmix and deflate the meringue.

4. Fold the melted butter into the meringue mixture until combined.

5. Using an offset spatula, spread the batter evenly onto the prepared sheet pan.

6. Bake for 5 to 7 minutes, or until evenly browned.

7. Transfer the cake, along with the parchment paper, to a wire rack and let cool for about 5 minutes. Roll up the cake with the parchment still attached and let cool completely. This will prevent the cake from cracking when you fill it with buttercream.

8. In a small saucepan over medium-high heat, mix together the remaining 200 grams of sugar and the water and bring to a boil. Lower the heat to medium-low and cook until the sugar is completely dissolved.

9. Unroll the cake and, using a pastry brush, brush it with the simple syrup.

To make the buttercream

1. Melt the chocolate in a double boiler.

2. Pour the melted chocolate into one of the bowls of buttercream and mix until completely combined. Set aside.

To assemble the yule log

1. Spread the cake with an even layer of vanilla buttercream.

2. Roll the cake into a log. Frost the log with the chocolate buttercream, making lines in the buttercream to resemble wood.

3. Cut about 3 inches off the end of the roll and attach it to the top of the main roll to resemble a cut branch.

4. Drag a fork along the buttercream to provide additional texture, and finish with decorations of your choice.

Upgrade Tip: Add fruit compote on top of the buttercream before you roll it to add another layer of flavor. My favorite compote to add is cranberry.

Substitution Tip: If you'd like to make a chocolate version of the cake, substitute 30 grams of cocoa powder for 30 grams of flour.

Chocolate Flourless Cake

Prep time: 30 minutes * **Cook time:** 25 to 30 minutes

A truly decadent dessert, this flourless chocolate cake is very dense and rich—exactly how a chocolate dessert should be. A small sliver will be more than enough to satisfy any sweet tooth. * *Yield: 1 (6-inch) cake*

58 grams unsalted butter, plus more for greasing the pan

40 grams almond flour, plus more for flouring the pan

40 grams semisweet chocolate, chopped

2 large eggs, separated

75 grams granulated sugar

1. Preheat the oven to 350°F. Butter and flour a 6-inch cake pan and line it with parchment paper.

2. In a double boiler over medium heat, melt the butter and chocolate and stir to combine. Remove from the heat.

3. Add the almond flour and egg yolks and stir to combine. Set aside.

4. In the bowl of a stand mixer fitted with the whisk attachment, whisk the sugar and egg whites until the mixture reaches stiff peaks.

5. Gently fold the meringue into the chocolate mixture and immediately pour into the prepared cake pan.

6. Bake for 25 to 30 minutes, or until a toothpick inserted in the center of the cake comes out mostly clean. It's okay to have a bit of moisture on your toothpick.

7. Set the cake aside to cool completely in the pan.

8. To unmold, place a serving plate over the cake pan and flip. Remove the cake pan and serve.

Troubleshooting Tip: The cake will fall as it's cooling. That's normal. Use a springform pan if you don't want to flip the cake and have the bottom be on top.

Serving Tip: Dust with a light coating of confectioners' sugar and decorate with fresh berries.

Boston Cream Pie Cupcakes

Prep time: 2 hours

I've always found this dessert name to be curious. Is it a pie or is it a cake? In the end, it's delicious and that's all that really matters. This cupcake version is a nice change of pace. • *Yield: 12 to 13 cupcakes*

For the frosting

340 grams semisweet
  chocolate chopped

30 grams corn syrup

215 milliliters heavy cream

For the cupcakes

1 recipe Pastry Cream
  (page 46)

½ recipe Vanilla Cake
  (page 110), made
  as cupcakes

To make the frosting

1. In a medium bowl, combine the chocolate and corn syrup.

2. In a small saucepan over medium heat, warm the heavy cream until small bubbles form around the edges of the pot. Pour the hot cream over the chocolate and let it sit for 2 minutes. Stir until the chocolate is completely melted, then let cool. Refrigerate for 1 hour.

To assemble the cupcakes

1. Whisk the pastry cream until it loosens up. Fill a pastry bag fitted with a round tip with the pastry cream.

2. Using a small paring knife, cut a hole in the top of each cupcake to remove a bit of the center.

3. Pipe pastry cream into the hole of each cupcake and top with the cut-out tops.

4. Fill another piping bag fitted with a decorative tip, such as Ateco #844, with the chocolate ganache. Pipe the ganache onto the top of the cupcakes and serve.

5. Store fully assembled cupcakes in an airtight container in the refrigerator for up to 24 hours. Let them come to room temperature before serving.

Technique Tip: You can buy cupcake corers at kitchen stores and online to make filling cupcakes quick and easy. You can also use an apple corer in a pinch.

Carrot Cake with Cream Cheese Frosting

Prep time: 15 minutes • **Cook time:** 30 to 35 minutes

A slice of carrot cake counts as a serving of veggies, right? Carrot cake was never high on my list of desserts until this recipe changed my mind. It's light, moist, and super flavorful. • *Yield: 1 (6-inch) 2-layer cake*

Butter, for greasing the pans

125 grams cake flour, plus more for dusting

1½ teaspoons ground cinnamon

½ teaspoon baking powder

½ teaspoon baking soda

½ teaspoon salt

½ teaspoon ground ginger

¼ teaspoon ground nutmeg

2 large eggs

420 grams granulated sugar, divided

85 milliliters vegetable oil

165 grams grated carrots

60 grams chopped walnuts, plus more for decorating

60 grams dried cranberries

250 grams crushed pineapple, drained

236 milliliters water

1 recipe Cream Cheese Frosting (page 107)

1. Preheat the oven to 350°F. Butter and flour 2 (6-inch) cake pans and line them with parchment paper.

2. In a medium bowl, sift together the flour, cinnamon, baking powder, baking soda, salt, ginger, and nutmeg and set aside.

3. In the bowl of a stand mixer, combine the eggs and 220 grams of sugar and whisk on medium speed until the mixture turns pale and creates a ribbon when it drips off the whisk.

4. With the mixer on, slowly drizzle the oil down the side of the bowl.

   PRO TIP: Be sure to add the oil slowly or the egg mixture may break and separate.

5. Add the flour mixture and mix just until combined.

6. Fold in the carrots, walnuts, dried cranberries, and crushed pineapple.

7. Pour the batter equally into the cake pans and bake for 30 to 35 minutes, or until a toothpick inserted into the center of the cake comes out clean.

8. Unmold the cakes immediately and let cool completely on a wire rack.

To assemble the cake

1. In a small saucepan over medium-high heat, mix together the remaining 200 grams of sugar and the water and bring to a boil. Lower the heat to medium-low and cook until the sugar is completely dissolved.

2. Using a serrated knife, cut each cake layer horizontally in half, leaving you with 4 layers.

3. Brush the cut side of each cake layer with the simple syrup.

4. Place 1 cake layer, cut-side up, on a cake round or serving plate.

5. Spread a ½-inch-thick layer of cream cheese frosting over the cake layer.

6. Repeat with the remaining layers. Spread a thin crumb coat of frosting all around the cake and place it in the refrigerator for at least 20 minutes.

7. Remove the cake from the refrigerator and spread with frosting until the cake is evenly covered.

8. Transfer any leftover frosting into a piping bag fitted with a decorative tip and pipe designs on top of the cake. If desired, coat the sides of the cake with additional chopped walnuts.

Strawberries and Cream Cupcakes

Prep time: 2 hours • Cook time: 12 to 15 minutes

Strawberries are one of the most beloved fruits. They make these indulgent cupcakes a great choice for a birthday or other type of celebration. • *Yield: 12 to 13 cupcakes*

For the cupcakes

100 grams strawberries
Granulated sugar
½ recipe Vanilla Cake
  (page 110) cupcake batter

For the whipped cream

2 sheets gelatin
450 milliliters heavy cream
100 grams confectioners' sugar
Fresh strawberries, for garnish

To make the cupcakes

1. In a blender, purée the strawberries until smooth. Transfer the strawberry purée to a small saucepan and cook over low heat until the mixture reduces to about 65 grams. Add sugar, 1 teaspoon at a time, until it reaches your desired sweetness. Set aside to cool for at least 1 hour.

2. Once the purée has cooled, preheat the oven to 325 °F. Line a cupcake pan with paper liners.

3. Add the purée to the cupcake batter and mix until combined.

4. Fill the cupcake liners with batter and bake for 12 to 15 minutes, or until a toothpick inserted into the center of the cake comes out clean. Let cool on a wire rack.

To make the whipped cream and assemble the cupcakes

1. In a shallow bowl, soak the gelatin in cold water.

2. Gently squeeze any excess moisture from the gelatin. Place the softened gelatin in a microwave-safe bowl and heat until melted, about 30 seconds.

3. In the bowl of a stand mixer fitted with the whisk attachment, combine the heavy cream, confectioners' sugar, and gelatin and whisk until it reaches stiff peaks.

4. Fill a piping bag fitted with a decorative tip with the whipped cream and pipe it onto the cooled cupcakes. Top with a fresh strawberry.

Blueberry Lemon Cupcakes

Prep time: 15 minutes • **Cook time:** 12 to 15 minutes

Blueberries and lemon are a wonderful flavor duo and these cupcakes showcases the combination's light and refreshing mixture of tangy sweetness. They have an almost muffin-like quality, so don't feel guilty about serving them for breakfast. • *Yield: 12 to 13 cupcakes*

For the cupcakes

½ recipe Vanilla Cake
   (page 110) cupcake batter
100 grams blueberries, plus
   more for decorating

For the glaze

120 grams confectioners' sugar
30 milliliters freshly squeezed
   lemon juice, plus more
   as needed
Fresh blueberries, for garnish

To make the cupcakes

1. Preheat the oven to 325°F. Line a cupcake pan with paper liners.

2. Add the blueberries to the vanilla cupcake batter.

   PRO TIP: Dust the blueberries with a little bit of flour before mixing into the batter to keep them from sinking to the bottom of the cupcakes while they are baking.

3. Fill the cupcake liners with batter and bake for 12 to 15 minutes, or until a toothpick inserted into the center of the cake comes out clean. Let cool on a wire rack.

To make the glaze and assemble the cupcakes

1. In a small bowl, mix together the confectioners' sugar and lemon juice, adding more lemon juice as needed to reach your desired consistency.

2. Using a spoon, pour the glaze over each cupcake and add a few fresh blueberries on top.

Chapter Six

Cookies and Bars

Florentine Cookies, page 142 (left)

Tips of the Trade

Most cookie and bar recipes are pretty straightforward. It's the subtle nuances that make a recipe that much better, especially in recipes that are so simple to begin with. Keep these tips in mind when making these recipes, and I think you'll see the difference.

Brown Butter

Any time a recipe calls for melted butter, I usually make it a point to brown the butter first. This will add another layer of rich, nutty flavor to your baked goods. You can store browned butter in an airtight container in the refrigerator to have on hand at any time.

To make brown butter: In a small saucepan over medium heat, melt your desired amount of butter. As the butter continues to cook, it will begin to foam, which will then subside. Little brown specks will form at the bottom of the pan, and the butter will start to give off a nutty aroma. Remove it from the pan and place it in a bowl to stop the cooking process, and allow it to cool down.

Use a Cookie Scoop

If you're like me, you prefer your cookies to be as evenly sized as possible, especially if you are serving them for special occasions or if you're giving them away as a gift. A cookie scoop will become your new best friend. A tried-and-true method, this ensures that not only will your cookies all come out the same size, but they'll also all cook at the same rate. Cookie scoops come in several sizes; I like the 2-inch scoop, which I think makes the perfect-size cookie.

Chill the Dough!

Chilling the dough is always a good idea because it helps the fats in the dough or batter firm up again, thus allowing them to melt slowly when baking. If your cookies have ever come out flat, it can be because your dough was too warm to begin with and the fats inside the dough had already started melting.

Store with a Slice of Bread

This is a fun trick I learned before I ever started baking on my own. If you place a slice of bread in the container with your cookies, the moisture from the bread will keep the cookies moist and chewy longer. A slice of white bread is best, as it will not transfer any unwanted flavor to your cookies.

Make Dough Ahead of Time

This tip goes hand in hand with chilling your dough. If you make your dough ahead of time and leave it in the refrigerator, you'll be ready to make cookies at almost any time. Wrap the dough tightly with plastic wrap for optimal storage. Also, most cookie and bar doughs can be frozen for several months. Remember to thaw the dough in the refrigerator overnight before you plan to use it.

Brown Butter Shortbread Cookies

Prep time: 45 minutes · **Cook time:** 16 to 18 minutes

The brown butter in this recipe really gives these shortbread cookies an extra boost of nutty, rich flavor. While these cookies are amazing on their own, I also like to add toffee bits, chopped pistachios, or chopped dried fruit to give them an extra boost of flavor. Add more or fewer add-ins, depending on your personal preference. Perfect with a cup of coffee or tea, this is a great cookie to keep on hand. · *Yield: 24 cookies*

225 grams unsalted brown
   butter (see page 132)
100 grams granulated sugar
55 grams dark brown sugar
320 grams all-purpose flour
¼ teaspoon salt
Demerara sugar, for topping
1 large egg, beaten, for
   egg wash

Optional Add-Ins

50 grams toffee bits
50 grams chopped
   pistachio nuts
50 grams chocolate chunks
50 grams dried cranberries
½ to 1 teaspoon orange zest
1 vanilla bean, scraped, or
   1½ teaspoons vanilla extract
   or paste

1. In the bowl of a stand mixer fitted with the paddle attachment, combine the brown butter, granulated sugar, and dark brown sugar and mix at medium speed until light and fluffy.

2. With the mixer on low, add the flour and salt and mix just until combined. If you are using any add-ins, mix them in at this point.

3. Transfer the dough to a clean work surface. If there are any pockets of flour that didn't get mixed in properly, knead the dough gently until incorporated.

4. Divide the dough in half and roll each piece into a log, about 6 inches long and 2 inches in diameter. Wrap each log in plastic wrap and refrigerate for at least 1 hour, until the dough is firm.

5. Preheat the oven to 350°F. Line 2 sheet pans with parchment paper. Place the demerara sugar in a wide shallow plate.

6. Brush the dough logs with the egg wash and roll them in the demerara sugar.

7. Using a serrated knife, cut the dough into ½-inch-thick slices and place them on the prepared sheet pan.

8. Bake for 16 to 18 minutes, or until the edges are browned. Let the cookies cool completely on a wire rack.

9. You can make the dough ahead of time, wrap it tightly in plastic wrap, and refrigerate for up to 1 week or freeze for several weeks. Baked cookies can be stored in an airtight container at room temperature for up to 2 weeks.

Linzer Cookies

Prep time: 1 hour 30 minutes • **Cook time:** 10 to 12 minutes

You can customize these beautiful cookies to be any shape and size you'd like. The combination of sweet jam and buttery crust is perfect for any cookie lover. • *Yield: 12 cookies*

281 grams unsalted butter,
  at room temperature
135 grams granulated sugar
240 grams all-purpose flour,
  plus more for dusting
168 grams almond flour
¼ teaspoon ground cinnamon
⅛ teaspoon ground nutmeg
130 grams raspberry jam
Confectioners' sugar,
  for dusting

1. In the bowl of a stand mixer fitted with the paddle attachment, combine the butter and sugar and mix on medium-high speed until light and fluffy, about 3 minutes.

2. Add 120 grams of all-purpose flour, the almond flour, cinnamon, and nutmeg and mix on low until combined. Add the remaining 120 grams of all-purpose flour in two batches and mix on low until fully combined.

3. Divide the dough in half, shape into disks, wrap each portion in plastic wrap, and chill for 1 hour.

4. Preheat the oven to 325°F. Line 2 sheet pans with parchment paper.

5. On a clean, lightly floured work surface, roll out one of the disks of dough to about ⅛ inch thick.

6. Using a 3-inch round cookie cutter, cut out as many pieces of dough as you can. You should have about 12 cookies. Transfer them to one of the prepared sheet pans and place in the refrigerator. These will be the bottoms of the linzer cookies.

7. Repeat the process with the second half of the dough, cutting out the dough with the 3-inch cookie cutter but also using a 1½-inch cookie cutter to cut the center out of each circle to create rings. Place the rings of dough on the second sheet pan and refrigerate for at least 15 minutes. These will be the tops of the linzer cookies.

8. Remove the sheet pans from the refrigerator and immediately bake for 10 to 15 minutes, or until the cookies are lightly browned.

9. Let the cookies cool completely on a wire rack.

10. Spread the jam on each of the bottom cookies and top with the cookie rings. Dust with confectioners' sugar.

11. The cookies can be stored in an airtight container at room temperature for up to 2 days.

Sesame Cookies

Prep time: 20 minutes • Cook time: 15 minutes

Sesame seeds in a cookie? You bet, and I promise these are some of the best cookies you'll ever try. I love sesame seeds and I'm always looking for new ways to incorporate them into recipes. What better way than in a cookie, right? • *Yield: 20 to 22 cookies*

80 grams sesame seeds

200 grams all-purpose flour

80 grams almond flour

½ teaspoon baking soda

150 grams unsalted butter,
  cubed, at room temperature

105 grams light brown sugar

1 large egg

½ teaspoon almond extract

1. In a small skillet over low heat, toast the sesame seeds, stirring frequently, until they begin to turn brown and become fragrant. Watch carefully because the seeds can burn very easily. Transfer the seeds to a bowl to cool.

2. In a medium bowl, whisk together the all-purpose flour, almond flour, and baking soda and set aside.

3. In the bowl of a stand mixer fitted with the paddle attachment, combine the butter and brown sugar and mix on medium speed until light and fluffy, about 2 minutes. Add the egg and almond extract and mix, scraping down the sides of the bowl, until well combined.

4. With the mixer on low, slowly add the flour mixture and mix just until the dough forms. Wrap the dough in plastic wrap and refrigerate for 20 minutes.

5. Preheat the oven to 350°F. Line a sheet pan with parchment paper.

6. Shape the dough into 25-gram balls and place them on the sheet pan. Using a glass, press each ball of dough flat, about ¼ inch thick. Cover each cookie with toasted sesame seeds, using your fingers, if necessary, to press the sesame seeds into the dough so that they stick.

7. Bake for 15 minutes, or until the cookies are golden brown.

8. Let the cookies cool completely on the sheet pan. They will become crunchy as they cool.

9. Store the cookies in an airtight container at room temperature for up to 1 week or frozen for up to 1 month.

Cranberry-Orange Oatmeal Cookies

Prep time: 30 minutes • **Cook time:** 12 to 14 minutes

Am I the only one who reaches for an oatmeal cookie when I want something sweet but want to feel like I'm still being healthy? These cookies are super delicious with lots of chewy texture, perfect for a morning snack or an afternoon treat. • *Yield: 30 to 34 cookies*

470 grams all-purpose flour

1 tablespoon ground cinnamon

1 teaspoon baking soda

1 teaspoon baking powder

1 teaspoon salt

Zest of 1 orange

236 grams unsalted butter, at room temperature

472 grams dark brown sugar

2 large eggs

2 teaspoons vanilla extract

710 grams rolled oats

250 grams dried cranberries

125 grams walnuts, chopped (optional)

1. In a medium bowl, whisk together the flour, cinnamon, baking soda, baking powder, salt, and orange zest and set aside.

2. In the bowl of a stand mixer fitted with the paddle attachment, combine the butter and brown sugar and mix on medium speed until light and fluffy, about 2 minutes.

3. Add the eggs, 1 egg at a time, and mix, making sure to incorporate each one fully. Add the vanilla and mix to combine.

4. With the mixer on low, slowly add the flour mixture until it is well combined and you no longer see any streaks of flour.

5. Add the oats, dried cranberries, and walnuts (if using) and mix until fully combined. Cover the bowl with plastic wrap and refrigerate for 20 minutes.

6. Preheat the oven to 350°F. Line a sheet pan with parchment paper.

7. Using a cookie scoop, measure out scoops of dough and place them on the prepared sheet pan, spacing them at least 2 inches apart to give them room to spread while baking.

8. Bake for 12 to 14 minutes, or until golden brown.

9. Let the cookies cool for a few minutes on the sheet pan before transferring them to a wire rack to cool completely.

Substitution Tip: Instead of dried cranberries and orange zest, try 60 grams of chocolate chips, 250 grams of dried blueberries, 125 grams of chopped pecans, or 250 grams of rum raisins.

Molasses Gingersnaps

Prep time: 1 hour 15 minutes • **Cook time:** 8 to 10 minutes

These spicy and sweet cookies are a holiday favorite, and they're made even more delicious with the addition of chewy crystallized ginger. The best part, though, is that you can make them in a snap! • *Yield: 20 to 24 cookies*

270 grams all-purpose flour

2 teaspoons baking soda

1 teaspoon ground ginger

1 teaspoon ground cinnamon

½ teaspoon allspice

½ teaspoon salt

170 grams unsalted butter, at
  room temperature

100 grams granulated sugar,
  plus more for rolling

110 grams dark brown sugar

1 large egg

85 grams unsulfured molasses

92 grams crystallized
  ginger, chopped

1. In a medium bowl, whisk together the flour, baking soda, ginger, cinnamon, allspice, and salt and set aside.

2. In the bowl of a stand mixer fitted with the paddle attachment, combine the butter, granulated sugar, and dark brown sugar and mix on medium speed until light and fluffy, scraping down the sides of the bowl, about 2 minutes.

3. Add the egg and molasses and mix until well incorporated.

4. With the mixer on low, slowly add flour mixture and mix until just combined. Fold in the crystallized ginger pieces until dispersed throughout.

5. Form the dough into a ball, wrap it in plastic wrap, and refrigerate for at least 1 hour, or until the dough is firm.

6. Preheat the oven to 350°F. Line a sheet pan with parchment paper. Pour some granulated sugar into a small bowl.

7. Form the dough into 1-inch balls and roll them in the sugar. Place them on the prepared sheet pan.

8. Bake for 8 to 10 minutes, or until the cookies begin to slightly crack. Transfer the cookies to a wire rack and let cool completely.

9. Store in an airtight container at room temperature for up to 4 days or freeze for up to 3 months.

Vegan Peanut Butter Cookies

Prep time: 10 minutes • **Cook time:** 8 minutes

Whether you're vegan or not, these cookies are fantastic. Bonus: Without eggs in the recipe, you can eat the raw dough safely. No one will know these tasty cookies are dairy-free. • *Yield: 15 to 20 cookies*

270 grams peanut butter

48 grams all-purpose flour

135 grams granulated sugar

62 grams applesauce

1½ teaspoons baking soda

1 teaspoon vanilla extract

¼ teaspoon salt

1. Preheat the oven to 350°F. Line a sheet pan with parchment paper.

2. In a microwave-safe bowl, heat the peanut butter in the microwave just enough to loosen it up, 15 to 20 seconds.

3. In the bowl of a stand mixer fitted with the paddle attachment, combine the peanut butter, flour, sugar, applesauce, baking soda, vanilla, and salt and mix until combined into a stiff dough.

4. Form the dough into 1-inch balls and place them on a prepared sheet pan, making sure to space them at least 1 inch apart.

   PRO TIP: To make each cookie the same size, use a kitchen scale to weigh each ball of dough before placing it on the sheet pan.

5. Bake for 8 minutes. Transfer the cookies to a wire rack to cool completely. The cookies may appear underdone when you remove them from the oven, but they will continue to firm up while they cool.

Substitution Tip: If you'd like to make these cookies gluten-free, as well, use rice flour instead of all-purpose flour.

Matcha–White Chocolate Chip Cookies

Prep time: 40 minutes • **Cook time:** 8 to 10 minutes

If you've never used matcha as an ingredient, you're missing out. The slightly bitter matcha in this cookie pairs perfectly with the creamy sweetness of white chocolate. Chewy and delicious, these cookies are just what you need when you're in the mood for something a little different. • *Yield: 24 cookies*

250 grams all-purpose flour

10 grams baking-grade matcha powder

1 teaspoon baking soda

1 teaspoon salt

170 grams unsalted brown butter (see page 132)

150 grams dark brown sugar

70 grams granulated sugar

1 large egg

1 large egg yolk

1 teaspoon vanilla extract

150 grams white chocolate, chopped

1. In a medium bowl, whisk together the flour, matcha, baking soda, and salt.

2. In the bowl of a stand mixer fitted with the paddle attachment, combine the butter, brown sugar, and granulated sugar and mix at medium speed until light and fluffy, about 2 minutes.

3. Add the egg, egg yolk, and vanilla and mix at medium speed until the mixture becomes lighter in color.

4. Fold in the flour mixture until just combined. Add the white chocolate and stir until combined. Cover the bowl with plastic wrap and refrigerate for 20 minutes.

5. Preheat the oven to 350°F. Line a sheet pan with parchment paper.

6. Using a cookie scoop, measure out scoops of dough and place them on the prepared sheet pan, spacing them at least 1 inch apart to give them room to spread while baking.

7. Bake for 8 to 10 minutes, or until the edges become slightly brown but the centers are still soft. Transfer the cookies to a wire rack and cool completely. The cookies will firm up as they cool.

Florentine Cookies

Prep time: 35 minutes • **Cook time:** 10 minutes

The first time I ever made these cookies, they were a huge hit, and now everyone asks me to make them every holiday season. They're crispy and slightly chewy, and they have the perfect chocolate-to-cookie ratio. * *Yield: 40 cookies, for 20 cookie sandwiches*

200 grams rolled oats

200 grams granulated sugar

150 grams unsalted brown butter (see page 132)

80 grams all-purpose flour

78 grams light corn syrup

57 milliliters whole milk

1 teaspoon vanilla extract

¼ teaspoon salt

340 grams milk chocolate or semisweet chocolate

1. Preheat the oven to 375°F. Line a sheet pan with parchment paper.

2. In the bowl of a stand mixer fitted with the paddle attachment, combine the oats, sugar, brown butter, flour, corn syrup, whole milk, vanilla, and salt and mix until well combined.

3. Using a tablespoon, scoop the batter onto to the prepared sheet pan leaving about 3 inches between cookies. Flatten the batter and make them as even as possible. This will ensure an even and crisp bake. You will need to bake the cookies in batches.

4. Bake for about 10 minutes, or until the cookies are golden brown and the centers are cooked through. Let them cool on the pan for 3 or 4 minutes, then transfer the cookies to a wire rack and cool completely.

5. Repeat the process until all the batter is gone.

6. In a double boiler, melt the chocolate until smooth.

7. Using a small offset spatula, spread the melted chocolate on the flat side of one cookie and sandwich it with a second cookie. Repeat with the rest of the cookies and serve.

8. Store in an airtight container at room temperature for up to 3 days.

Salted Chocolate–Chocolate Chunk Cookies

Prep time: 15 minutes　•　**Cook time:** 8 to 10 minutes

There are a million chocolate chip cookie recipes around, so I decided to do something a little different. This cookie elevates the flavors we've come to love with the addition of cocoa powder and flaky sea salt. Rich and chewy with a slight crispiness, these are some of the best cookies you'll ever bake.　•　*Yield: 20 to 24 cookies*

165 grams all-purpose flour

60 grams unsweetened cocoa powder

1 teaspoon baking soda

½ teaspoon espresso powder

¼ teaspoon salt

220 grams light brown sugar

168 grams unsalted butter, at room temperature

1 large egg

1 teaspoon vanilla extract

220 grams semisweet chocolate, chopped

Flaky sea salt, for topping

1. In a medium bowl, sift together the flour, cocoa powder, baking soda, espresso powder, and salt and set aside.

2. In the bowl of a stand mixer fitted with the paddle attachment, combine the brown sugar and butter and mix on medium speed until light and fluffy, about 2 minutes.

3. Add the egg and vanilla and mix until well incorporated.

4. With the mixer on low, add the flour mixture and mix until just combined. The dough will be thick.

5. Fold in the chocolate chunks until combined. Cover the bowl with plastic wrap and refrigerate for 10 to 15 minutes, until it firms up a bit.

6. Preheat the oven to 350°F. Line a sheet pan with parchment paper.

7. Using a cookie scoop, measure out scoops of dough and place them on the prepared sheet pan, spacing them at least 1 inch apart to give them room to spread while baking. Sprinkle a bit of sea salt on top of each cookie.

8. Bake for 8 to 10 minutes, until the edges are cooked. The centers will look a little underdone.

9. Transfer the cookies to a wire rack and let them cool completely. They will firm up as they cool.

10. Store the cookies in an airtight container at room temperature for up to 1 week. Uncooked dough can be wrapped tightly in plastic wrap and stored in the refrigerator for up to 3 days.

Chocolate-Dipped Macaroons

Prep time: 15 minutes • **Cook time:** 15 to 20 minutes

Moist, chewy, and bathed in chocolate, these macaroons are also gluten-free. They are a wonderful treat that comes together very quickly. Bring them to a potluck or take them to a picnic. • *Yield: 20 to 30 macaroons*

300 grams unsweetened
  shredded coconut
150 grams granulated sugar
100 grams large egg whites
1 teaspoon vanilla extract or
  almond extract
½ teaspoon salt
170 grams
  semisweet chocolate

1. In the bowl of a stand mixer, combine the coconut, sugar, egg whites, vanilla, and salt and mix together until combined.

2. Preheat the oven to 250°F. Line a sheet pan with parchment paper.

3. Using a cookie scoop, measure out scoops of dough and place them on the prepared sheet pan.

4. Bake for 15 to 20 minutes, or until the macaroons are lightly browned. Transfer them to a wire rack to cool completely.

5. In a double boiler, melt the chocolate and stir until smooth.

6. Dip the bottoms of the cookies into the chocolate. Wipe off any excess, place on the sheet pan, and let set.

7. Store the macaroons in one layer in an airtight container and refrigerate for up to 3 days.

Madeleines

Prep time: 10 minutes　•　**Cook time:** 5 to 7 minutes

Some consider these cookies, while others consider them little cakes. Either way, they're beautiful and delicious, and you should definitely make them for a brunch or an elegant dessert. ◦ *Yield: 24 cookies*

250 grams granulated sugar

220 grams all-purpose flour, plus more for dusting

1 teaspoon baking powder

Zest of 2 lemons

½ teaspoon salt

4 large eggs

220 grams unsalted butter, melted, plus more for greasing the pans

Confectioners' sugar, for dusting

1. In the bowl of a stand mixer fitted with the paddle attachment, combine the sugar, flour, baking powder, lemon zest, and salt and mix on medium speed until incorporated.

2. Add the eggs, one at a time, making sure they're each incorporated well.

3. Add the melted butter and mix just until combined. Be careful not to overmix.

4. Fill a pastry bag fitted with a round tip with the batter and chill until it's firm, about 1 hour.

5. Preheat the oven to 400°F. Butter and flour 2 (12-cup) madeleine pans.

6. Pipe the chilled batter into the prepared pans.

7. Bake for 5 to 7 minutes, or until they are set and spring back to the touch.

8. Unmold immediately onto a wire rack and sprinkle with confectioners' sugar.

9. Madeleines don't store well, so serve them the same day you make them.

Technique Tip: You can make the batter up to 2 days ahead and refrigerate until ready to use.

Substitution Tip: Change the flavors by using different citrus zests or flavored extracts.

Palmiers

Prep time: 35 minutes • Cook time: 15 to 20 minutes

These cookies have many names, including "elephant ears," which is what I called them when I was growing up. Palmiers are so incredibly delicious, crispy, and crunchy, offering the perfect combination of buttery sweetness. I could literally eat a dozen of these cookies in one sitting and not even think twice about it. • *Yield: 25 to 30 cookies*

Granulated sugar, for dusting
200 grams Puff Pastry
   (page 48)

1. Sprinkle a generous amount of granulated sugar over a clean work surface.

2. Roll out the dough on top of the sugar to a 13-by-13-inch square about ⅛ inch thick. Sprinkle more sugar over the top.

3. Fold two opposite sides toward the center with each side folded halfway to the center. Fold the sides again so that they meet at the center of the dough. Then fold the dough in half as though closing a book.

4. Gently press the layers together with a rolling pin. Wrap the dough in plastic wrap and chill until firm, about 20 minutes.

5. Preheat the oven to 350°F. Line a sheet pan with parchment paper.

6. Cut the folded dough into ⅜-inch-thick slices and place them on the prepared sheet pan.

7. Bake for 8 to 10 minutes. Flip the slices with a spatula and bake for another 7 to 10 minutes, until they are browned evenly on both sides.

8. Palmiers are best eaten the same day they are made, but you can store them in an airtight container at room temperature for up to 2 days.

Technique Tip: Be really generous with the sugar. You want to make sure there is enough to cover the dough really well.

Troubleshooting Tip: Leave plenty of space between the cookies on the sheet pan because they will almost double in size while baking.

Fudge Brownies

Prep time: 15 minutes • **Cook time:** 35 to 40 minutes

I don't know why anyone makes brownies from a boxed mix when they are so easy to make from scratch. This recipe is exactly what you want when you're craving a traditional fudgy brownie. Try swirling in some peanut butter, raspberry jam, caramel, or toffee chips for a change of pace. • *Yield: 20 to 24 brownies*

150 grams unsweetened
   cocoa powder

136 grams all-purpose flour

28 grams espresso powder

1 teaspoon salt

534 grams granulated sugar

340 grams unsalted
   butter, melted

4 large eggs

220 grams semisweet
   chocolate, chopped

1. Preheat the oven to 350°F. Line a 9-by-13-inch baking pan with parchment paper, leaving a bit of overhang on each end. This will make it easier to remove the brownies from the pan.

2. In a small bowl, sift together the cocoa powder, flour, espresso powder, and salt and set it aside.

3. In a medium bowl, whisk together the sugar and melted butter until well combined. Add the eggs and mix to combine.

4. Add the flour mixture in three batches, making sure to fully incorporate each batch. Fold in the chopped chocolate.

5. Pour the batter into the prepared pan and bake for 35 to 40 minutes. Let the brownies cool on a wire rack completely. Cut into squares.

6. Store in an airtight container at room temperature for up to 3 days or wrapped individually in plastic wrap and frozen for up to 1 week.

Upgrade Tip: If you'd like to add different flavors, fold in ingredients like toffee chips or nuts after you add the flour mixture. To swirl in peanut butter, caramel, or jam, warm it in the microwave for about 30 to 45 seconds to loosen it up. After the brownie batter is poured into the pan, dollop the ingredient in different spots and use a butter knife to swirl it through the batter.

Carmelita Bars

Prep time: 30 minutes • **Cook time:** 35 to 40 minutes

Full of different flavors and textures, these bars are incredibly decadent and chewy and have a gooey middle that makes them irresistible. Just between us, the edges and corners are the best part! • *Yield: 20 to 24 bars*

For the crust

240 grams all-purpose flour

227 grams unsalted
  butter, melted

150 grams dark brown sugar

100 grams rolled oats

60 grams sweetened
  shredded coconut

1 teaspoon baking soda

½ teaspoon salt

For the filling

284 grams caramel
  candy pieces

28 milliliters whole milk

170 grams semisweet
  chocolate, chopped

150 grams pecans, chopped

To make the crust

1. Preheat the oven 350°F. Line a 9-by-13-inch baking pan with parchment paper, leaving a bit of overhang on each end. This will make it easier to remove the bars from the pan.

2. In a medium bowl, mix together the flour, butter, brown sugar, oats, coconut, baking soda, and salt.

3. Spread half of the mixture into the prepared pan, pressing it evenly in the pan, especially at the edges and corners. Bake for 10 minutes. Let cool on a wire rack. Set aside the remainder of the crust mixture.

To make the filling and assemble the bars

1. In a medium saucepan over medium heat, combine the caramel and milk and cook, stirring constantly, until the caramel is melted.

2. Spread the caramel onto the baked crust and let sit for 15 to 20 minutes, until the caramel looks less shiny and appears firmer.

3. Sprinkle the chocolate and pecans over the cooled caramel. Spread the remaining crust mixture over the top and press lightly.

4. Bake for 25 to 30 minutes, or until the edges are bubbling and the top is lightly browned.

5. Let cool completely in the pan before removing and cutting into bars.

6. Store in an airtight container at room temperature for up to 5 days or wrap them individually in plastic wrap and freeze for up to 1 month.

Technique Tip: You can also melt the caramel with the milk in the microwave by heating it in 20 second intervals, stirring in between, until it's melted.

Brown Butter Blondies

Prep time: 20 minutes • **Cook time:** 25 to 30 minutes

You know by now that I'm a chocolate fanatic, and I will always pick chocolate when given the choice. Chocolate is everything. But sometimes a blondie just hits the spot. Nutty from the brown butter and perfectly sweet, these bars can make even the most die-hard chocolate lover rethink their choice. • *Yield: 20 to 24 bars*

240 grams all-purpose flour

1 teaspoon baking powder

½ teaspoon salt

200 grams dark brown sugar

170 grams unsalted brown
    butter (see page 132)

150 grams granulated sugar

2 teaspoons vanilla extract

2 large eggs, at
    room temperature

165 grams white
    chocolate, chopped

125 grams macadamia nuts,
    chopped (optional)

1. Preheat the oven to 350°F. Line a 9-by-13-inch baking pan with parchment paper, leaving a bit of overhang on each end. This will make it easier to remove the blondies from the pan.

2. Sift the flour, baking powder, and salt into a medium bowl.

3. In the bowl of a stand mixer fitted with the paddle attachment, combine the brown sugar, brown butter, granulated sugar, and vanilla and mix on low speed until just combined. Add the eggs, one at a time, until fully incorporated.

4. Add the flour mixture and mix until combined. Fold the chocolate and nuts (if using) into the batter.

5. Spread the batter into the prepared pan in an even layer and bake for 25 to 30 minutes, or until golden brown. Let cool completely in the pan before cutting into bars.

6. Store in an airtight container at room temperature for up to 5 days or wrap them individually in plastic wrap and freeze for up to 1 month.

Apple Pie Bars

Prep time: 30 minutes • Cook time: 35 minutes

It doesn't get much better than apple pie, or does it? These bars give you all the flavor of a traditional apple pie, but with less fuss. For a little something extra, serve them with a scoop of ice cream or drizzle of caramel sauce. • *Yield: 20 to 24 bars*

For the filling

4 apples peeled, cored, and cubed (see Technique Tip)
75 grams light brown sugar
30 grams unsalted butter
Juice of ½ lemon
1 vanilla bean, split and scraped, or 1½ teaspoons vanilla extract
1 tablespoon ground cinnamon
½ teaspoon ground ginger
¼ teaspoon ground nutmeg
¼ teaspoon salt
25 milliliters water

For the crust

230 grams unsalted brown butter (see page 132), melted
100 grams granulated sugar
2 teaspoons vanilla extract
½ teaspoon salt
265 grams all-purpose flour

For the streusel

140 grams dark brown sugar
120 grams cold unsalted butter, cubed
80 grams rolled oats
60 grams all-purpose flour
½ teaspoon ground cinnamon

To make the filling

In a large saucepan over medium heat, combine the apples, brown sugar, butter, lemon juice, vanilla, cinnamon, ginger, nutmeg, salt, and water and cook until the apples are tender. Remove from the heat and set aside.

To make the crust

1. Preheat the oven to 325°F. Line a 9-by-13-inch baking pan with parchment paper, leaving a bit of overhang on each end. This will make it easier to remove the bars from the pan.

2. In a medium bowl, mix together the brown butter, sugar, vanilla, and salt. Add the flour and mix to combine. Press the dough evenly into the baking pan.

3. Bake for 15 minutes, or until golden brown.

To make the streusel and assemble the bars

1. Raise the oven temperature to 350°F.

2. In the bowl of a stand mixer fitted with the paddle attachment, combine the brown sugar, butter, oats, flour, and cinnamon and mix on low speed until the mixture is crumbly. Set aside.

3. Spread the apple filling in an even layer over the crust. Sprinkle the streusel mixture over the top. Bake for 20 minutes, or until the top is nicely browned. Let cool completely in the pan before cutting into bars.

4. Store in an airtight container at room temperature for up to 3 days or wrap them individually in plastic wrap and freeze for up to 1 month.

Technique Tip: Use a combination of sweet apples, such as Honeycrisp or Golden Delicious, and tart ones, like Granny Smith or Pink Lady.

Strawberry Cheesecake Bars

Prep time: 15 minutes • **Cook time:** 45 minutes

Here is the best recipe for cheesecake lovers. These bars are creamy and sweet with a crisp chocolate crust; a small bite will satisfy your sweet tooth. • *Yield: 20 to 24 bars*

For the crust

230 grams unsalted
   butter, melted

100 grams granulated sugar

2 teaspoons vanilla extract

½ teaspoon salt

150 grams all-purpose flour

115 grams cocoa powder

For the filling

678 grams cream cheese, at
   room temperature

200 grams granulated sugar

2 large eggs

56 grams sour cream

1 teaspoon vanilla extract

125 grams strawberry
   jam, warmed

To make the crust

1. Preheat the oven to 350°F. Line a 9-by-13-inch baking pan with parchment paper, leaving a bit of overhang on each end. This will make it easier to remove the bars from the pan.

2. In a medium bowl, mix together the butter, sugar, vanilla, and salt. Add the flour and cocoa powder and mix until just combined. Press the dough into the baking pan as evenly as possible.

3. Bake for 12 minutes, or until the center is set. Set aside to cool.

To make the filling and assemble the bars

1. In the bowl of a stand mixer fitted with the paddle attachment, mix the cream cheese and sugar at medium speed until smooth. Add the eggs, one at a time, mixing well after each addition. Add the sour cream and vanilla and mix until smooth.

2. Pour the mixture onto the cooled crust and spread evenly.

3. Drop dollops of the warmed jam over the top of the filling. Using a knife, swirl the jam into the cheesecake filling.

4. Bake for 30 minutes, or until the edges are lightly browned and the center jiggles slightly. Let the bars cool in the pan completely. Refrigerate for at least 1 hour, until the filling is set.

5. Store the bars in an airtight container for up to 5 days.

Substitution Tip: Use the crust from the Raspberry Lemon Bars (page 153) if you prefer a shortbread crust to a chocolate crust. You can also switch up the flavors by using different flavors of jam to swirl into the filling.

Raspberry Lemon Bars

Prep time: 10 minutes • **Cook time:** 1 hour

A step up from the traditional lemon bar, the addition of raspberries makes these a big hit at any party or gathering. Super tangy with a sweet finish and a buttery crust, these bars are everything you could possibly want in a sweet treat. • *Yield: 20 to 24 bars*

For the crust

265 grams all-purpose flour

230 grams unsalted
butter, melted

100 grams granulated sugar

2 teaspoons vanilla extract

½ teaspoon salt

For the filling

375 grams frozen
raspberries, thawed

306 milliliters freshly squeezed
lemon juice

345 grams granulated sugar

167 grams all-purposed flour

Zest of 3 lemons

6 large egg whites

2 large eggs

¼ teaspoon salt

Confectioners' sugar,
for dusting

To make the crust

1. Preheat the oven to 325°F. Line a 9-by-13-inch baking pan with parchment paper, leaving a bit of overhang on each end. This will make it easier to remove the bars from the pan.

2. In a medium bowl, mix together the flour, butter, sugar, vanilla, and salt until just combined. The dough will be thick. Press the mixture into the prepared baking pan as evenly as possible.

3. Bake for 18 to 20 minutes, or until lightly browned.

To make the filling and assemble the bars

1. Place the raspberries in a fine-mesh strainer over a bowl. Using a spatula, press the berries to extract as much juice and pulp as you can. Discard the seeds. Add the lemon juice to the raspberry pulp and stir to combine. Set aside.

2. In the bowl of a stand mixer fitted with the paddle attachment, combine the sugar, flour, lemon zest, egg whites, eggs, and salt and mix on medium speed until just combined. Add the raspberry-lemon mixture and mix until smooth.

3. Pour the filling into the baked crust and bake for 35 to 40 minutes, or until the center is set and no longer jiggles. Let cool in the pan until firmly set before cutting into bars and sprinkling with confectioners' sugar.

4. The bars can be stored in an airtight container in the refrigerator for up to 1 week.

Chapter Seven

Décor

*Croquembouche, page 56 (left), decorated
with spun sugar and violas*

Decorating with Chocolate

Chocolate is one of the most popular things to decorate with, and there are several ways of using it to embellish cakes, pies, and other pastries.

Tempering Chocolate

If you want chocolate decorations that are shiny, smooth, and have that sharp "snap" when it breaks, you need to temper it. This is the process of heating, cooling, and agitating chocolate, which breaks down its molecular structure and creates a more stable crystalline structure. Tempered chocolate is also less likely to melt at room temperature.

How to Temper Chocolate

There are three ways to temper chocolate: tabling, ice bath, and seeding.

Tabling. For this method, pour heated (to the proper temperature, listed in the following table) chocolate on a smooth, clean work surface. Using metal scrapers, continuously scrape the chocolate from the edges toward the center, until it cools to the desired temperature.

Ice bath. Heat chocolate to the correct temperature. Place the bowl of heated chocolate over a bowl of water and ice and stir continuously to cool it down to the desired temperature. Be mindful not to get any water in the chocolate or it will seize up and you will have to start over with new chocolate.

Seeding. This is the easiest and most foolproof method, in my opinion. In a small saucepan, heat chocolate to the correct temperature. Add small pieces of already tempered chocolate (in the form of store-bought chocolate chips or bars) and gently stir until all of the chocolate is melted and cools to the temperature listed in the following table.

TYPE OF CHOCOLATE	HEAT TO	COOL TO
Dark chocolate	122°F	81°F
Milk chocolate	113°F	79°F
White chocolate	113°F	79°F

Abstract Chocolate Designs

The great thing about abstract designs is that they are always super fun to make and there's no right or wrong way to make them. Simply pour some tempered chocolate onto a plastic acetate sheet and let it set. Pour a different kind of melted chocolate over the designs and, using a spatula, smooth it across the designs. Let the chocolate set. When the chocolate has hardened, peel off the acetate and break the chocolate into randomly shaped pieces. Use them to decorate cakes or cupcakes.

Chocolate Leaves

Chocolate leaves are a beautiful addition to any cake or tart, and they can also be used as a simple garnish to a plated dessert. They're also super simple to make. Simply take a pastry brush, dip it into melted tempered chocolate, and brush the underside of any kind of edible, shiny leaf that hasn't been treated with any sort of pesticides. (Lemon leaves are a great choice.) Add a few layers of chocolate, making sure each layer has set before adding a new one. Once you're satisfied with the thickness and the chocolate has set, slowly peel the leaf off the chocolate from the stem.

Chocolate Piped Designs

It's quite easy to make your own designs simply by piping whatever shapes or lines you'd like to use. Line a sheet pan with parchment paper. Fill a paper cornet (essentially a piping bag made of paper) with melted tempered chocolate or candy melts and pipe whatever shapes you'd like, such as stars, butterflies, hearts, or swirls. Let them set and apply them on top of your cakes, cupcakes, or a slice of a tart.

Sugar Work

Another great way to incorporate simple décor into your desserts is by using different sugar techniques. Not only does it add an extra sweetness to your dessert, but it also adds texture by providing something crunchy on the plate. You can also add gel food coloring to sugar to change it to whatever colors you'd like.

Please use caution when handling sugar. The temperatures are extremely hot, and it is quite easy to burn yourself from splashes.

How to Make Spun Sugar

In a medium saucepan over medium heat, combine 500 grams of sugar, 156 grams of corn syrup, and 113 milliliters of water. Cook, using a wet pastry brush to clean the sides of the pot if needed, until it reaches 300°F on a candy thermometer. Remove from the heat and place over a water bath. Let cool to 275°F. You're now ready to work with the sugar.

Sugar Cages

Oil the outside of a small bowl. I also like to use the back of a ladle (it depends on how big you'd like the cage). Dip a fork into the prepared hot sugar and quickly drizzle it across the top of the bowl or spoon, continuously moving it in different directions. Let cool. These are perfect for placing on top of circular desserts or for using as an edible bowl when flipped over.

Sugar Spirals

Line a sheet pan with parchment paper and coat it lightly with oil. Using a spoon, drizzle the sugar into a spiral shape on the parchment and let set. It's now ready to add to any dessert or cake. Use this method to make any kind of shape or design you like.

Isomalt

Isomalt is a sugar product that many pastry chefs and cake makers use to create beautiful sugar decorations. With more home bakers delving into the world of sugar art, isomalt is readily available to purchase at your local cake supply store or online. It's super easy to use, too. All you need to do is follow the ratio of isomalt to water found on the package and boil it until you reach the proper temperature on a candy thermometer. While isomalt is edible, it doesn't offer much in the way of flavor. Unlike traditional sugar, it is not hydroscopic, so it won't suck in any moisture, which can ruin sugar decorations if the weather is humid. This makes isomalt perfect for decorations no matter the environment you work in, and you can color it whatever hues you like.

Isomalt Bubbles

To make these easy decorations, line a sheet pan with parchment paper. Color isomalt beads as desired and place them on the sheet pan, arranging them in any kind of organic shape you'd like. Bake at 350°F for 3 to 4 minutes, until they are melted and form bubbles throughout. Let the sugar pieces cool completely before using. These decorations are incredibly beautiful but extremely delicate. They're perfect for placing directly on top of a cupcake or a slice of cake.

Isomalt Molds and Pours

Melted isomalt can be poured into candy molds to create beautiful transparent decorations. Try piecing together different molded pieces. For instance, if you have two flat butterfly wings but you'd like to create some dimension with your decorations, use a kitchen torch to slightly heat the edges of the wings and piece them together to create a three-dimensional butterfly. You can also pour isomalt into cutouts in cookies or use them in gingerbread houses to create stained-glass windows.

Cake Decorating

Cake decorating is a huge love of mine and really what started my whole culinary journey. There are so many different techniques and ways to incorporate themes and color schemes into your designs that it would take another book to get through them all. Here are some basics to get you started. With a little practice, the sky's the limit.

Frosting Your Cake

This is one of the most, if not *the* most, important part of building and decorating your cake. Whether you choose to cover a cake in buttercream or fondant, all cakes should have a buttercream crumb coat. This is the application of a thin layer of buttercream all over the cake that prevents cake crumbs from getting into the more decorative layers on top. After you apply the crumb coat, refrigerate the cake for at least 30 minutes before adding more layers of buttercream or applying any other decorations. I use an offset spatula and a bench scraper as my main tools when I'm frosting a cake. I use the offset spatula to apply the buttercream to the cake and smooth it around to make sure I have an even amount all the way around. I then use my bench scraper, holding it vertically and parallel to the cake, to scrape away the excess buttercream around the cake, while simultaneously smoothing out the sides. At that point, you can continue to decorate as you desire.

Buttercream Flowers

Flowers made out of buttercream are some of the most beautiful decorations you can make for a cake. I always begin by coloring my basic white buttercream with gel food coloring and letting the colors sit for at least 12 to 24 hours. I find that the longer the colors have time to meld with the buttercream, the more intense they are. I use Swiss Meringue Buttercream (page 104) for all of my decorations. It has a lovely texture and tastes delicious. It's a little delicate, so I refrigerate it frequently for about 5 minutes at a time while I'm working to prevent it from getting too soft and melting. For step-by-step instructions on how to make flowers, *100 Buttercream Flowers* by Valeri Valeriano and Christina Ong is a great resource, as is Wilton's YouTube channel for online tutorials. Buttercream flowers take a lot of practice, but they're so much fun that you'll be a pro in no time. I use these Ateco piping tips when making flowers: 61, 104, 120, 122, 127, 143, 401, 349 (leaf).

Fondant

Fondant can add a really polished and clean look to your cakes. You can buy it ready-made, and my go-to fondant is made by Satin Ice. It's a wonderfully consistent product that makes working with it a lot less intimidating. The best way to ensure that fondant will go on a cake smoothly is to make sure your buttercream base is smooth and even. Roll out the fondant as thin as possible and about 1½ times larger than the size you need. As you're covering the cake, make sure that you're using a fondant smoother to simultaneously smooth out the surface. Cut off any excess fondant that has gathered at the bottom. Sometimes bubbles get trapped underneath the fondant—just use a sterilized sewing pin to pop them.

Embellishments

Often, it's the final touches that really bring everything together and make everyone go, "Wow!" The following are some ideas of ways to easily elevate your desserts.

Edible Flowers

Edible pansies, lavender, violets, and roses, among others, bring a whimsical look and splash of color to desserts (see cover photo of Naked Cake with Ganache Drip, recipe on page 112, decorated with scented geraniums, violas, alyssum, blackberry flowers, and dianthus). While these flowers are indeed edible, you may not actually want to eat them because many of them can be slightly bitter. To counter that, dip them in water, sprinkle them with sugar, and let them dry before adding them to your baked good. Be sure to purchase only organic flowers free of pesticides.

Luster Dust and Edible Glitter

Luster dust and glitter are beautiful ways to add color and dimension to your desserts. You can use them to add some sparkle to cakes or the top of a smooth chocolate ganache tart. They're also perfect for using with a brush to dust onto chocolate or sugar decorations.

Edible Gold and Silver Leaf

Just a little bit of gold or silver leaf goes a long way. Using these is a really simple technique to elevate any dessert or cake. They add a sense of luxury and decadence to any dish. I especially love to use gold or silver leaf on small, simple desserts, like macarons or chocolate truffles. Using food-grade tweezers, take a small amount of gold or silver leaf and place it on top. If you want to use gold or silver leaf on a buttercream cake, just press the sheet against the side of the cake and it should stick. If your cake is covered in fondant, brush a thin layer of piping gel (my favorites are from Wilton or AmeriColor) on the cake and apply it in small sections.

*Raspberry Chocolate Ganache Tart, page 91,
decorated with fresh raspberries, freeze-dried
raspberries, and quince blossoms*

Measurement Conversions

Volume Equivalents (Liquid)

US STANDARD	US STANDARD (OUNCES)	METRIC (APPROXIMATE)
2 tablespoons	1 fl. oz.	30 mL
¼ cup	2 fl. oz.	60 mL
½ cup	4 fl. oz.	120 mL
1 cup	8 fl. oz.	240 mL
1½ cups	12 fl. oz.	355 mL
2 cups or 1 pint	16 fl. oz.	475 mL
4 cups or 1 quart	32 fl. oz.	1 L
1 gallon	128 fl. oz.	4 L

Oven Temperatures

FAHRENHEIT (F)	CELSIUS (C) (APPROXIMATE)
250°F	120°C
300°F	150°C
325°F	165°C
350°F	180°C
375°F	190°C
400°F	200°C
425°F	220°C
450°F	230°C

Volume Equivalents (Dry)

US STANDARD	METRIC (APPROXIMATE)
⅛ teaspoon	0.5 mL
¼ teaspoon	1 mL
½ teaspoon	2 mL
¾ teaspoon	4 mL
1 teaspoon	5 mL
1 tablespoon	15 mL
¼ cup	59 mL
⅓ cup	79 mL
½ cup	118 mL
⅔ cup	156 mL
¾ cup	177 mL
1 cup	235 mL
2 cups or 1 pint	475 mL
3 cups	700 mL
4 cups or 1 quart	1 L

Weight Equivalents

US STANDARD	METRIC (APPROXIMATE)
½ ounce	15 g
1 ounce	30 g
2 ounces	60 g
4 ounces	115 g
8 ounces	225 g
12 ounces	340 g
16 ounces or 1 pound	455 g

Resources

AmeriColor
americolorcorp.com

Ateco
atecousa.com

Satin Ice
satinice.com

Wilton (for supplies)
wilton.com

Wilton (for decoration tutorials)
youtube.com/user/wiltoncakedecorating/videos

Index

Page locators in **bold** indicate pictures

Acknowledgments

To Andy, without your thoughtfulness, this wouldn't have been possible. To my editor Rebecca, for making me feel like writing this book was a lot easier than it actually was. Your support and guidance helped me more than you know.

To all of my instructors at ICC, whose brilliance and passion not only inspired me but also changed my life forever.

To my friends, who have cheered me on throughout this process. Your excitement and encouragement helped push me through.

Lastly, to my family. Mom and Dad, for always being there, even when I don't think I need you. Joe, my brother, for your endless support and for providing my greatest inspirations in life, Amelia, Ava, and JoJo. My sister Joelle, for reminding me how beautiful and sparkly my soul really is. I couldn't have done this without you. CK, for being the constant in my life.

Thank you all.

About the Author

 **Jaclyn Rodriguez** is a pastry chef and teaching visual artist who combines her love for everything creative by creating edible art in the form of decorated cakes. Since starting her own cake business, Cake Designs by Jaclyn, in 2017, she has continued to share her love of art and pastry with her growing following.

Jaclyn received her Grand Diplôme with Distinction in Professional Pastry Arts from the famed International Culinary Center. Jaclyn lives in New York City and revels in living in one of the world's most exciting culinary cities.

CPSIA information can be obtained
at www.ICGtesting.com
Printed in the USA
BVHW051405160720
583793BV00003B/3